AT. Support

# PRACTICE IN ESSENTIAL SKILLS

# ENGLISH ONE

A. Abbott & D. O'Sullivan



COLLINS
EDUCATIONAL

# Alphabetical Order

Alphabetical Order is the order of letters in the alphabet.

a b c **d** e f g h i j k l m n o **p** q r s **t** u **v** w x y z

A B C **D** E F G H I J K L M N O **P** Q R S **T** U **V** W X Y Z

d comes before p which comes before t and v

**Example 1** Arrange these names in alphabetical order for a school register:

| | | |
|---|---|---|
| **H**arris | H comes before S but after B | **B**right |
| **S**andhu | S comes after H and B | **H**arris |
| **B**right | B comes before H and S | **S**andhu |

**A** If the first letter is the same we have to look at the second letter.

**Example 2** Arrange the names of these towns in alphabetical order:

| | | |
|---|---|---|
| B**o**urnemouth | They all begin with B, so look | B**a**rnsley |
| B**u**rnley | at the second letters. | B**o**urnemouth |
| B**r**ighton | **a** comes first, then **o**, next **r** | B**r**ighton |
| B**a**rnsley | and finally **u**. | B**u**rnley |

**B** If the first two letters are the same we have to look at the third letter.

**Example 3** Arrange the names of these roads in alphabetical order:

| | | |
|---|---|---|
| Co**o**per Road | All begin with Co, so look | Co**b** Road |
| Co**i**n Road | at the third letters. | Co**i**n Road |
| Co**l**in Road | **b** comes first, followed by | Co**l**in Road |
| Co**b** Road | **i**, **l** and **o** and finally **u.** | **Coo**per Road |

**Exercise 1**
Arrange these school subjects in alphabetical order:

Science — Geography
English — French
Mathematics

**Exercise 2**
Arrange these composers in alphabetical order:

Bach — Britten
Berlioz — Bartok
Brahms — Bellini
Beethoven

**Exercise 3**
Arrange these English counties in alphabetical order:

Norfolk — Northamptonshire
Surrey — Sussex
Somerset — Northumberland
Suffolk — Nottinghamshire

**Exercise 4**
Using the map printed opposite place the towns listed in alphabetical order.

**Exercise 5**
Find one word beginning with the letter **p** for:

**1** a jewel **2** a job **3** a country **4** a sport **5** a town
**6** a fish **7** a bird **8** an animal **9** a vegetable **10** a flower
**11** a colour **12** a fruit **13** a tree **14** a first name **15** a surname

# The Dictionary

A dictionary will help you find out what a word means.

It will also tell you the correct way of spelling a word.

Dictionaries are set out in alphabetical order.

mat comes before match, mate and material,
lad comes before ladder, lady and lake.

These definitions are taken, in a shortened form, from *Collins Gem Dictionary*.

Notice that the words are in alphabetical order.

Where a word has more than one meaning, these are given.

**Exercise 1**
In your dictionary, find the pages that contain each of the following words. Write down the meaning of each one.

**1** addition **2** subtraction **3** division **4** multiplication

**Exercise 2**
At first, it may take you a long time to find the words you want. The more you use a dictionary, the faster you will get. Time how long it takes you to find the following words. Write down one meaning for each word:

**1** laboratory **2** conclusion **3** apparatus **4** diagram **5** radiation
**6** density **7** acid **8** filter **9** tongs **10** volume

# Verbs (1)

A verb expresses an action or a state of being.

**A** Generally a verb is a "doing" word: jump, cry, tell.

**Example 1** The verbs are underlined in this story:
The teacher strolled into the room and closing the door, sat down. When he saw Maria hanging from the light-fittings he flew into a rage and screamed at her. I laughed and he shouted at me too. When he calmed down, Maria and I apologised for what we had done.

**B** Often a verb tells us that someone **is** or **was**, **will be**, **could be**, **were** or **are**.

**Example 2** He **is** a boy. I **am** quiet. The teacher **is** a lunatic. They **were** alone in the room. I **will be** happy tomorrow. They **are** silly.

**Exercise 1**
Copy and then underline the verbs in these sentences:

1 We study Geography at school.
2 Lava flows from a volcano.
3 More rain falls in Scotland than England.
4 The River Thames flows from the Cotswold Hills to the North Sea.
5 Coal is mined in Yorkshire, Kent and South Wales.
6 Ships load and unload in docks.
7 Leeds is to the north of Birmingham.
8 Britain is an island.
9 The English Channel separates France and England.
10 Britain consists of Wales, Scotland and England.

**Exercise 2**
For each letter of the alphabet give a verb.
For example, apply, beat, catch, and so on.

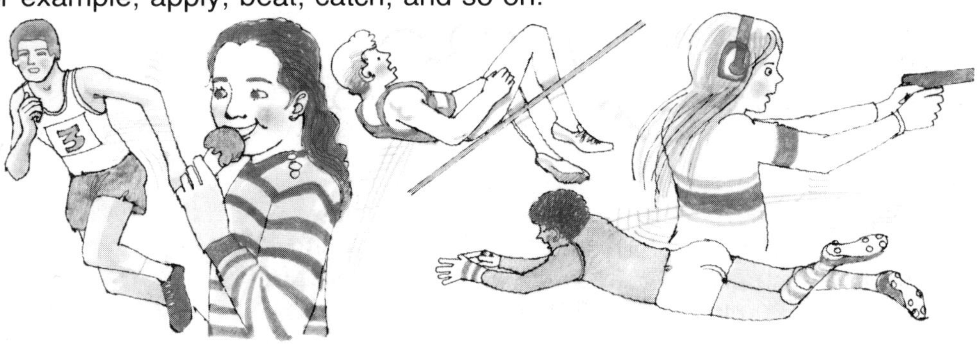

## Exercise 3

### War Between Signon and Luta

In this story of war, you decide what happens by choosing a verb from each set of brackets. In the first sentence you must decide if the Signons loved or hated war.

The Signons (loved/hated) violence. One day they (had to go/wanted to go) to war with their neighbours, the Lutans. The Lutans always (enjoyed/detested) fighting and they (relished/feared) the prospect of battle with the Signon Empire.

The Lutan King (suggested/demanded) that his forces (be prepared/be ordered) to (die/make peace) rather than (win/lose) the war. In the course of battle, the Signons (suffered/inflicted) serious injuries. Their king (dreaded/longed for) further reports from his fleet.

Now finish the story, underlining all the verbs you use.

## Exercise 4

### Words Similar in Meaning

Find one word that is similar in meaning to each of the following:

| | | | | |
|---|---|---|---|---|
| **1** abandon | **2** broad | **3** conceal | **4** astonish | **5** rude |
| **6** run | **7** empty | **8** copy | **9** spoke | **10** shouted |

# Sentences (1)

A sentence is a group of words which must make complete sense.

This is not a sentence: To boil an egg you must
This is a sentence: To boil an egg you must use boiling water.

**A** For a sentence to make complete sense you must use a verb.
Verbs express "doing" or "being".
These are verbs: fall, fell, feel, feed, finish, find, flick.

**B** All sentences begin with a capital letter.
Make sure that your capital letters are bigger than ordinary letters.
For example, Ff, Gg, Aa, Zz.

**C** All sentences end with a full stop.

*This is wrong* { boiling an egg is easy half fill a pan with water put the egg in the pan heat the water until it is boiling boil the egg for four minutes eat the egg.

*This is correct* { Boiling an egg is easy. Half fill a pan with water. Put the egg in the pan. Heat the water until it is boiling. Boil the egg for four minutes. Eat the egg.

**Exercise 1**
Copy and complete these sentences so that they make sense.
Be careful to copy out the capital letters and full stops.

**1** Geography is ______ study of the Earth's climate, land, seas and population.
**2** __________ is the capital ____ England.
**3** ______ highest mountain ____ Britain is Ben Nevis.
**4** Edinburgh ____ 608 miles ________ London.
**5** The west coast ____ England ______ more rainfall ________ the east coast.
**6** There ______ 47 counties ____ England.
**7** Around 20,000,000 sheep ______ __________ ____ Britain.
**8** The shortest distance ________ England ____ France is between Dover ______ Calais.
**9** Fuels ________ in England include gas, oil and ________.
**10** Barley, wheat ______ oats ______ grown ____ most __________ of England.

**Exercise 2**

Copy out these sentences and put in the capitals and full stops where they belong. Number 1 is done for you.

1 Scotland is in the north of Britain.
2 there are many small islands off the Scottish coast.
3 the north of Scotland has many mountains
4 Ben Nevis is the highest mountain
5 most people live in the lowland area
6 coal is mined near Glasgow
7 the capital city of Scotland is Edinburgh
8 fishing is important in the east of Scotland
9 lakes in Scotland are known as lochs
10 The River Spey is the longest Scottish river

**Exercise 3**

In this recipe, the instructions have been mixed up.
Unscramble each sentence so that the recipe can be understood.

**Hamburgers to make how**

You need will 4 oz beef minced, onion, salt, pepper.
Butter in pan melt a the.
Pan in onion the fry the.
Mince the with the onion mix.
Pepper and salt mix the in.
The mixture pat a round into shape.
Until cooked fry mixture the it is.
Bun a toast roll or.
Hamburger inside the place roll the.

**Exercise 4**

Write as many sentences as you can about this picture.

**Exercise 5**

Write out each of the following examples and put in the full stops and capitals where they belong. The number of sentences in each example is given.

1 The founder of the Moslem religion was Mohammed he was born some time between the years 570 and 580 A.D. in Mecca (*two sentences*)

2 Mohammed was brought up by his grandfather and uncle he emerged as a prophet when he was forty (*two sentences*)

3 he stated the existence of one god the name of this god was Allah the religious leaders of Mecca did not accept Mohammed's message (*three sentences*)

4 he fled 200 miles to Medina here he became a religious, political and military leader In 630 his army conquered Mecca (*three sentences*)

5 he rebuilt the sacred temple he established Medina as the capital of the new Moslem state the Arabian chiefs vowed allegiance (*three sentences*)

6 the bible of Islam is the Koran it consists of the things Allah was said to have spoken to Mohammed it was not written down until after his death the Koran consists of 200,000 words it is divided into fourteen chapters (*five sentences*)

7 Allah is also called the Hearer and the Guide he is complete master of the Universe Allah created the earth and heaven in six days he will judge each person on the Day of Judgement (*four sentences*)

8 Jesus Christ appears in the Koran as a prophet he was a messenger of Allah the Koran insists Allah had no son Jesus is just a man (*four sentences*)

9 Prayer is an essential part of the Moslem religion it takes place five times a day a Moslem faces Mecca when praying (*three sentences*)

10 Fasting takes place during Ramadan this is the ninth lunar month of the year a Moslem should visit Mecca at least once in his life (*three sentences*)

**Exercise 6**

Recently an ancient city was discovered in the desert. On a stone wall there were some strange carvings. They were a form of early writing. The alphabet used is compared with our alphabet in the table below.

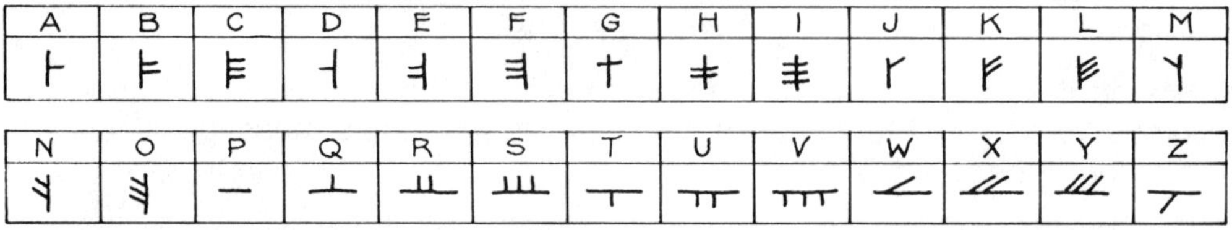


This ancient writing has no gaps between words, no capital letters and no punctuation, so it is very difficult to translate.

Try and put the riddle below in to organised, punctuated English and see if you can guess who is speaking (it's a kind of bird).

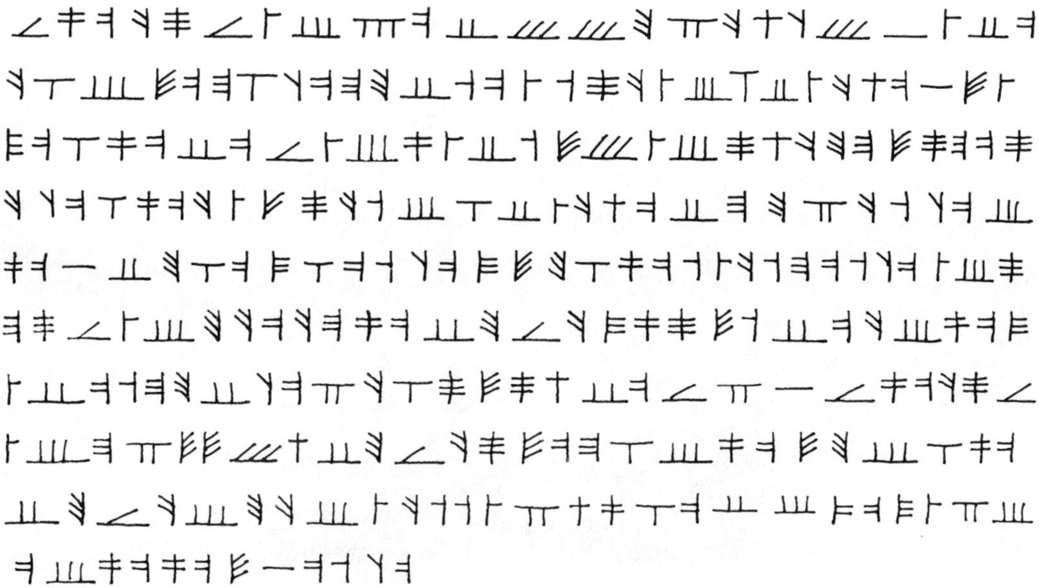

# Sentences (2)

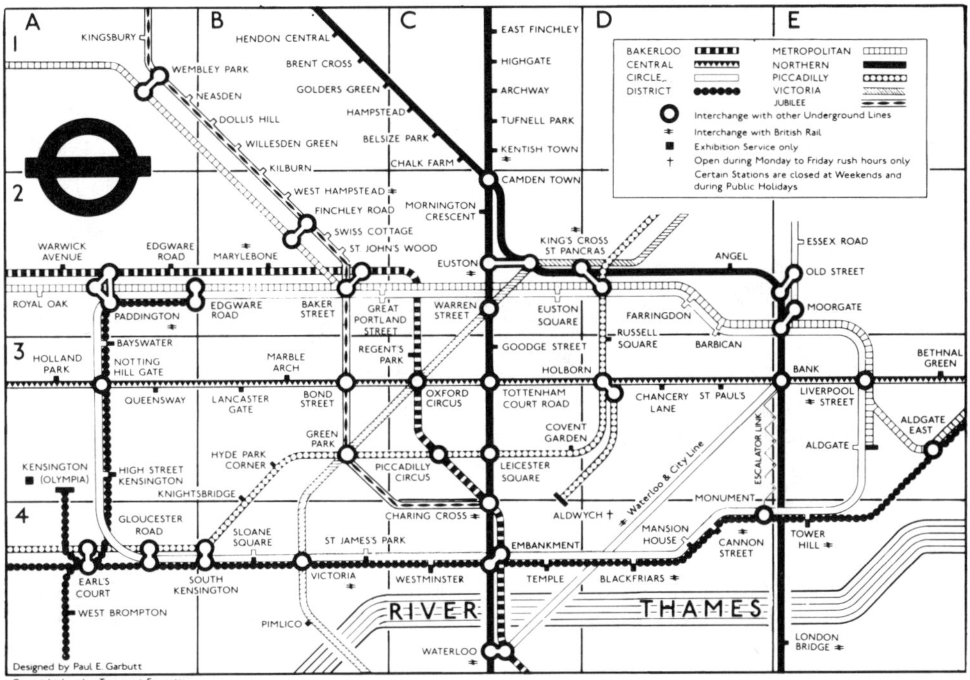




London Transport Underground Map, Registered User No. 83/064

STATIONS BOUNDED BY THE CIRCLE LINE

| Map Square | Station | Map Square | Station |
|---|---|---|---|
| E3 | ALDGATE | B3 | KNIGHTSBRIDGE |
| C3 | ALDWYCH | B3 | LANCASTER GATE |
| B2 | BAKER STREET | C3 | LEICESTER SQUARE |
| E3 | BANK | E3 | LIVERPOOL STREET |
| D2 | BARBICAN | D4 | MANSION HOUSE |
| A3 | BAYSWATER | B3 | MARBLE ARCH |
| D4 | BLACKFRIARS | D4 | MONUMENT |
| B3 | BOND STREET | E2 | MOORGATE |
| D4 | CANNON STREET | A3 | NOTTING HILL GATE |
| D3 | CHANCERY LANE | C3 | OXFORD CIRCUS |
| C4 | CHARING CROSS | A2 | PADDINGTON |
| C3 | COVENT GARDEN | C3 | PICCADILLY CIRCUS |
| B2 | EDGWARE ROAD | A3 | QUEENSWAY |
| C4 | EMBANKMENT | C3 | REGENT'S PARK |
| C2 | EUSTON SQUARE | D3 | RUSSELL SQUARE |
| D2 | FARRINGDON | B4 | ST. JAMES'S PARK |
| A4 | GLOUCESTER ROAD | D3 | ST. PAUL'S |
| C3 | GOODGE STREET | B4 | SLOANE SQUARE |
| B2 | GREAT PORTLAND STREET | B4 | SOUTH KENSINGTON |
| B3 | GREEN PARK | C4 | TEMPLE |
| A3 | HIGH STREET KENSINGTON | C3 | TOTTENHAM COURT ROAD |
| D3 | HOLBORN | E4 | TOWER HILL |
| B3 | HYDE PARK CORNER | B4 | VICTORIA |
| D2 | KING'S CROSS ST. PANCRAS | C2 | WARREN STREET |
| | | C4 | WESTMINSTER |

**Exercise 1**
Follow the directions below, and name the stations at which you arrive.

1 At South Kensington, take the Piccadilly Line going north and change at Green Park. Take the Victoria Line going north and change at Oxford Circus. The station you want is the next stop on the northbound Bakerloo line.

2 From Moorgate, take the Circle Line going west and change at King's Cross/St. Pancras. Travel two stops on the Piccadilly Line and change to the Central Line. The station you want is four stops along the Central Line, going west.

**Exercise 2**
Now give directions for the following journeys. Find out where the stations are first and then plan your route. Often you will have a choice of routes so choose the one that seems the shortest.

Give directions:
1 From Notting Hill Gate to Warren Street
2 From Marble Arch to Victoria
3 From Goodge Street to High Street Kensington
4 From Edgware Road to Oxford Circus
5 From Knightsbridge to Bank
6 From Russell Square to Regent's Park
7 From Westminster to Bond Street
8 From Bayswater to Covent Garden

# Question Marks

A sentence which asks a question has a question mark at its end.

**A** Questions often ask:
Who? When? Why? How? Did you? Can you?
What? Where? Which? Do you? Will you? Are you?

**Exercise 1**
Imagine that you are late for school. Copy out the following questions asked by your subject teacher. Write an answer for each question you are asked.

1. Who are you?
2. What class are you in?
3. Whose class is that?
4. Why are you late?
5. Where do you live?
6. When did you leave home?
7. How did you get here?
8. Did you miss the bus?
9. What kind of an excuse is that?
10. Are you mad?

**Exercise 2**
The following sentences are answers. Write out the questions which go with them.

1. The Romans first came to Britain in 55 B.C.
2. Their leader was Julius Caesar.
3. The most northerly position the Romans controlled was marked by Hadrian's Wall.
4. Hadrian's Wall was a line of forts from the Clyde to the Firth of Forth.
5. The Roman rule of Britain was opposed by Cardoc until 50 A.D., by Boadicea in A.D. 61, and by the Picts and the Celts.
6. The Romans' hold on Britain was weakened because they had to withdraw troops to fight in Rome.
7. The Romans abandoned control of Britain in 409 A.D.
8. They left behind fine roads, bridges, baths, villas and towns.
9. You can recognise some Roman towns because their names end in -caster or -chester (for example Winchester and Doncaster).
10. There is a Roman bath at Bath and a Roman theatre at St. Albans.

## Exercise 3

| | MONDAY | TUESDAY | WEDNESDAY | THURSDAY | FRIDAY |
|---|---|---|---|---|---|
| 9.05 – 9.45 | English | History | History | Home Economics | Religious Education |
| 9.45 – 10.25 | Religious Education | Physics | Physics | Home Economics | English |
| MORNING BREAK | | | | | |
| 10.45 – 11.25 | Geography | Music | French | Art | Mathematics |
| 11.25 – 12.05 | Mathematics | English | English | Mathematics | French |
| LUNCH BREAK | | | | | |
| 1.10 – 1.50 | Chemistry | Chemistry | Biology | Music | Art |
| 1.50 – 2.30 | French | Geography | Mathematics | French | Physical Education |
| 2.30 – 3.10 | Biology | Mathematics | Physical Education | English | Physical Education |

Answer these questions on the timetable shown above:

**1** How many lessons are there each day?
**2** How many English lessons does the class have in a week?
**3** What abbreviations are used for Physical Education and Religious Education?
**4** How long is spent in lessons in a week?
**5** What subject is studied in period 3 on Thursday?
**6** Why do you think Home Economics is a double lesson?
**7** Which subject is most likely not to have an examination?
**8** How long is the lunch break?
**9** Loukia likes English, Biology and History. What is her favourite day?
**10** Cathy likes French and Physical Education but dislikes Science subjects. What day does she like least?

**Exercise 4**

Copy out your own timetable and answer these questions:

1 How long is your lunch break?
2 How long do you spend in lessons each day?
3 What lesson do you have in period 4 on Tuesday (day 2)?
4 What subjects do you have before lunch on Thursday (day 4)?
5 In which room do you spend the most time?
6 What subjects are studied by the class in Exercise 3 that you do not study?
7 Which lesson is your favourite?
8 How many different lessons do you have?
9 Which of your present subjects did you study in your last school?
10 Would you prefer your timetable or the one in Exercise 3? Why?

**Exercise 5**

Using your timetable, provide questions for these answers:

**1** 9.30 a.m. **2** Monday. **3** Twice.
**4** Three. **5** After lunch on Thursday.

**Exercise 6**

**Instruments of the Orchestra**

The name of each of these musical instruments has been jumbled.
Re-arrange the letters in each word to form the correct name.

| **strings** | **brass** | **percussion** | **wind** | **keyboards** |
|---|---|---|---|---|
| lavio | brotmone | mudrs | eboo | nipao |
| linvio | nosexapah | sablycm | soonbas | ganro |
| locel | petrumt | angelrit | inclaret | hischapdorr |
| bledou sabs | norh hencrf | patminy | fetul | |
| tagriu | tenroc | inebourmat | | |

**Dictionary Exercise**

Use each of the following words in a sentence so that its meaning is clear:

**1** refund **2** withdraw **3** enclose **4** invite **5** subsequently
**6** recognise **7** emerged **8** proclaimed **9** politician **10** abbreviations

# Codes

**Morse code** was first used for sending telegraph messages. You can use a buzzer or torch to send the sounds or flashes that make up the message. Letters are made up of dots or dashes, or both of these together. The flash or buzz for a dash is three times longer than that for a dot.
This is what morse code looks like written down:

| | | | | | | | | | |
|---|---|---|---|---|---|---|---|---|---|
| A | . — | F | . . — . | K | — . — | P | . — — . | U | . . — |
| B | — . . . | G | — — . | L | . — . . | Q | — — . — | V | . . . — |
| C | — . — . | H | . . . . | M | — — | R | . — . | W | . — — |
| D | — . . | I | . . | N | — . | S | . . . | X | — . . — |
| E | . | J | . — — — | O | — — — | T | — | Y | — . — — |
| | | | | | | | | Z | — — . . |

### Exercise 1
Look at this message: . . . . . . . — . . . . — — .

Why is it difficult to decode? Try again with the letters separated.

. . . ./. /. — . ./. — — .

### Exercise 2
Try and decode this message:
. — —/. . . ./././— ./— . — —/— — —/. . —/. . ./././— — —/. — ./. . . ./././. —/
. — ./. —/— —/./. . ./. . ./. —/— —./././. . . ./— — —/. — —/— . ./— — —/— . — —/
— — —/. . —/— . —/— ./— — —/. — —/ . — —/. . . ./././— ./. —/. — . ./././—/—/./
. — ./— — —/. — ./. — — /— — —/. — ./— . ./././— ./— . ./. . ./. —/— ./— . ./
—/. . . ./././— ./././— . . —/—/. — . ./././—/—/./. — ./— — —/. — ./. — —/
— — —/. — ./— . ./— . . ./././— — ./. ./— ./. . ./?

### Exercise 3
Using your mouth as a buzzer, or in writing, send a message in morse code to the person next to you. You will have to invent a way to signal spaces between letters and words and perhaps also some simple punctuation.

### Exercise 4
1 Send a message using numbers for the letters of the alphabet.
  For example, a=1 b=2 c=3
  What does this say? 20–5–12–5–7–18–1–13
2 Reverse the alphabet so that a=z b=y c=x
  What does this say? gll nfxs
3 Invent your own code. Give a message to a partner and see if he or she can break it.

# Common Nouns and Proper Nouns

**A common noun** is the name of any person, place or thing. For example, pupil, teacher, classroom, laboratory, river, mountain.

**Exercise 1**
Give six common nouns for each of these general terms:
**1** fruit **2** vegetables **3** sports **4** jobs
**5** musical instruments **6** common nouns beginning with **st**

**Exercise 2**
Name all the common nouns in the picture below.

**A proper noun** is the name given to a particular person, place or thing so that we can tell it apart from all others.

For example, **M**r. **R**ashid told **S**ally to go to **E**uston **S**tation

| Mr. Rashid | Sally | Euston Station |
|---|---|---|
| ↓ | ↓ | ↓ |
| the man's name | the girl's name | the station's name |
| ↓ | ↓ | ↓ |
| proper noun | proper noun | proper noun |

For example, the **R**iver **S**evern is the longest river in **B**ritain.

proper noun — capital **R**, capital **S**
common noun — small **r**
proper noun — capital **B**

**Exercise 3**
For each of the following common nouns find a proper noun.
For example, **common noun** boy **proper noun** Emil Jones

| | | | | |
|---|---|---|---|---|
| **1** pupil | **2** teacher | **3** church | **4** day | **5** month |
| **6** river | **7** mountain | **8** ocean | **9** road | **10** town |
| **11** county | **12** country | **13** continent | **14** planet | **15** city |
| **16** writer | **17** politician | **18** train station | **19** queen | **20** singer |
| **21** book | **22** school | **23** T.V. show | **24** shop | **25** film |

**Exercise 4**
Rewrite this passage giving each proper noun capital letters. Remember, if a proper noun consists of two words (as does your name) each word begins with a capital letter.

William I, also known as william the conqueror, was king of england, 1066 to 1087. He was the son of robert, duke of normandy. William emerged from a long struggle with the king of france with control of normandy and other territories. He had been promised the english throne by his cousin edward the confessor and by harold who had been shipwrecked in france. When harold was proclaimed king of england william invaded england. At the battle of hastings in October 1066 harold was killed and the normans were victorious. The story of the norman conquest is told, from the norman point of view, in the bayeux tapestry. On christmas day william was crowned king of england in westminster abbey. England was not totally subdued for another five years until the defeat of hereward the wake.

# Singular Nouns and Plural Nouns

**A noun** is the name of a person, place or thing.
For example, these are nouns: girl, school, book.

**Singular** means **only one** of a person, place or thing.
For example, boy, teacher, house, station, desk, chair.

**Plural** means **more than one** of a person, place or thing.
For example, boys, teachers, houses, stations, desks, chairs.

**A** To find the plural of a word, we usually add **s**.
For example, pot**s**, pan**s**, oven**s**, apple**s**, egg**s**, cake**s**.

### Exercise 1

Give the plural of these words:

| | | | | |
|---|---|---|---|---|
| **1** horse | **2** cat | **3** dog | **4** pet | **5** bee |
| **6** elephant | **7** giraffe | **8** dolphin | **9** lion | **10** tortoise |

**B** To find the plural of a word ending in y we look at the letter before the y.
If the letter is a vowel (a, e, i, o, u), we add **s**.
For example, key becomes key**s**, day becomes day**s**.

If the letter before the y is not a vowel, we change the y to **i** and add **es**.
For example, family becomes famil**ies**, story becomes stor**ies**.

### Exercise 2

Give the plural of these words:

| | | | | |
|---|---|---|---|---|
| **1** army | **2** industry | **3** county | **4** play | **5** city |
| **6** century | **7** country | **8** day | **9** monkey | **10** energy |

**C** To find the plural of a word ending in **f** we change the **f** to **ve** and add **s**.
For example, calf becomes cal**ves**, thief becomes thie**ves**.

### Exercise 3

Give the plural of these words:

| | | | | |
|---|---|---|---|---|
| **1** wife | **2** knife | **3** shelf | **4** leaf | **5** half |
| **6** loaf | **7** life | **8** elf | **9** wolf | **10** scarf |

**D** To find the plural of words ending in s, x, z, sh or ch we add **es**.
For example, bus becomes bus**es**, match becomes match**es**.

**Exercise 4**

Give the plural of these words:

| | | | | |
|---|---|---|---|---|
| **1** dish | **2** switch | **3** kiss | **4** address | **5** six |
| **6** class | **7** watch | **8** buzz | **9** box | **10** ash |

**E** Some words do not follow these rules.

**Exercise 5**

Give the singular of these words:

| | | | | |
|---|---|---|---|---|
| **1** children | **2** teeth | **3** women | **4** sheep | **5** dice |
| **6** potatoes | **7** feet | **8** chiefs | **9** geese | **10** pianos |

**Exercise 6**

### Singular and Plurals Crossword

ACROSS
1 plural of fly *(5)*
6 plural of arm *(4)*
9 they fall in Autumn *(6)*
12 garden tool *(3)*
14 donkey *(3)*
15 less than two vets *(3)*
16 plural of man *(3)*
17 usual plural ending *(1)*
18 a short drink *(3)*

DOWN
2 plural of loaf *(6)*
3 elm trees *(4)*
4 plural of tax *(5)*
5 slippery fish *(3)*
7 yellows, oranges and . . . . *(4)*
8 plural of shelf *(7)*
10 ending of plural of class *(2)*
11 ringing clock *(5)*
13 singular of spies *(3)*
19 just one on the sink *(3)*

**Exercise 7**

Draw two columns in your exercise book.
In the left-hand column list each object you can see in your room at home.
In the right-hand column list the plurals of these objects.

# Verbs (2)
# Present Tense and Past Tense

**A verb** is an action word.
For example, make, play, paint, kick, fix.

**A** These verbs are in the **present tense** – the actions are being done now – at present.

**Exercise 1**
Write one sentence for each of the following verbs.
Each verb is in the present tense. Number 1 is done for you:

**1** The footballer **kicks** the ball into the goal.

| | | | | |
|---|---|---|---|---|
| **1** kicks | **2** throws | **3** punches | **4** runs | **5** smashes |
| **6** lobs | **7** catches | **8** fouls | **9** sprint | **10** jumps |
| **11** swings | **12** swims | **13** dives | **14** aims | **15** drives |
| **16** wrestles | **17** lifts | **18** rides | **19** leaps | **20** shoots |

In this paragraph, everything happens in the present tense:

I **walk** into the room and **see** a man standing there. He **is** about six feet tall and **has** a black beard. He **wears** a blue suit and **carries** a grey overcoat. I **ask** him what he **wants** and he **tells** me he **wants** to speak to my mother. He **says** that I should tell my mum that he **is** there. As I **leave** the room he **asks** me my name which I **tell** him. My mum **comes** in and he **tells** her that he **is** a policeman.

**B** Most books are written in the **past tense**. When writing stories or essays it is usual to write as if the events described have already happened – yesterday, last week or last year. We use the **past tense** to show that things have already happened.

| PRESENT TENSE | PAST TENSE |
|---|---|
| I **walk** into the room. | I **walked** into the room. |
| He **asks** me my name. | He **asked** me my name. |
| I **close** the door. | I **closed** the door. |

The previous passage about the policeman can be put into the **past tense** by changing the verbs in heavy type.

I **walked** into the room and **saw** a man standing there. He **was** about six feet tall and **had** a black beard. He **wore** a blue suit and **carried** a grey overcoat. I **asked** him what he **wanted** and he **told** me he **wanted** to speak to my mother. He **said** that I should tell my mum that he **was** there. As I **left** the room he **asked** me my name which I **told** him. My mum **came** in and he **told** her that he **was** a policeman.

**C** To form the past tense of a verb from its present tense often involves adding **-ed**. For example, ask – ask**ed**, walk – walk**ed**, punch – punch**ed**, smash – smash**ed**.

**Exercise 2**
Write a sentence using each of these verbs in the **past tense**:

| | | | | |
|---|---|---|---|---|
| **1** roar | **2** scream | **3** annoy | **4** scratch | **5** enjoy |
| **6** detest | **7** collect | **8** start | **9** destroy | **10** suggest |

**D** Verbs that end in **e** form the past tense by adding **d**.
For example, love – love**d**, hate – hate**d**, refuse – refuse**d**, arrive – arrive**d**.

**Exercise 3**
Write a sentence using each of these verbs in the **past tense**.

| | | | | |
|---|---|---|---|---|
| **1** hope | **2** like | **3** tease | **4** hire | **5** describe |
| **6** notice | **7** starve | **8** scare | **9** swerve | **10** accelerate |

The letters a, e, i, o and u are vowels.
**Short** vowels are sharp, quick sounds that appear to be squeezed in.
For example, h**i**t, d**i**p, b**e**g, r**u**n, c**a**p, m**a**p, t**o**p, p**o**t.

**E** To form the past tense of a verb ending in a short vowel followed by a consonant, we double the final consonant and add **ed**.
For example, drop – dro**pped**, dip – di**pped**, rub – ru**bbed**, regret – regre**tted**, slap – sla**pped**.

**Exercise 4**
Write a sentence using each of these verbs in the **past tense**:

| | | | | |
|---|---|---|---|---|
| **1** blot | **2** grab | **3** hop | **4** beg | **5** shop |
| **6** stop | **7** knit | **8** skid | **9** rip | **10** cap |

**F** To form the past tense of a verb ending with a consonant followed by **y**, we change the **y** to **i** and add **ed**.
For example, marry – marr**ied**, hurry – hurr**ied**, dry – dr**ied**, rely – rel**ied**, pity – pit**ied**.

**Exercise 5**
Write a sentence using each of these verbs in the **past tense**.

| | | | | |
|---|---|---|---|---|
| **1** carry | **2** supply | **3** spy | **4** apply | **5** reply |
| **6** deny | **7** study | **8** worry | **9** copy | **10** satisfy |

**G** There are many verbs that do not form their past tense in the way we would expect. These are **irregular verbs**.

**Exercise 6**
Copy out the table below, and fill in the gaps. Where you are given the present tense of a verb you must find the past tense. Where this is given you will need to write the present tense.

| PRESENT | PAST | PRESENT | PAST |
|---|---|---|---|
| —— | drank | buy | —— |
| sit | —— | bring | —— |
| —— | put | —— | caught |
| cut | —— | fight | —— |
| sing | —— | —— | did |
| —— | rang | get | —— |
| —— | flew | give | —— |
| know | —— | —— | dug |
| grow | —— | see | —— |
| —— | threw | speak | —— |
| draw | —— | —— | swore |
| win | —— | write | —— |
| —— | read | eat | —— |
| —— | ran | is | —— |
| lose | —— | —— | chose |

**Exercise 7**
Taking care to write in the **past tense**, write a story using one of these titles:

| | |
|---|---|
| **1** An interview with the police | **2** My last birthday |
| **3** The unwelcome guest | **4** Escape from school |
| **5** Danger on the beach | **6** Yesterday |

## Exercise 8

### Verb Crossword

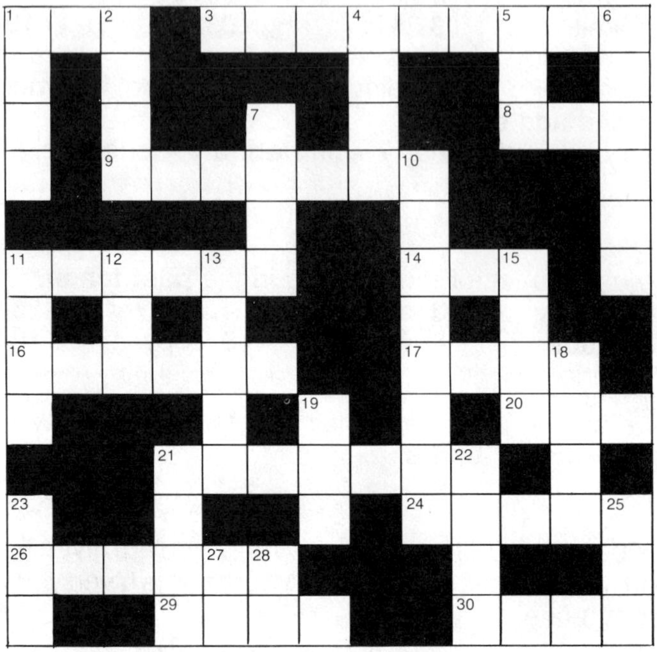

ACROSS

1 past tense of is *(3)*
3 past tense of signal *(9)*
8 to fasten *(3)*
9 they broke when I ________ them on the floor *(7)*
11 travelled on foot *(6)*
14 past tense of sit *(3)*
16 past tense of nod *(6)*
17 the weeds ____ wild in the garden last year *(4)*
20 past tense of do *(3)*
21 arrested *(7)*
24 she ______ the cards *(5)*
26 today is sunny, yesterday it ________ *(6)*
29 present tense of 17 across *(4)*
30 to ensnare *(4)*

DOWN

1 past tense of are *(4)*
2 replied, answered, spoke *(4)*
4 to jot things down on paper *(4)*
5 allow, or rent out *(3)*
6 past tense of dream *(6)*
7 past tense of speed *(4)*
10 drew plans *(8)*
11 past tense of go *(4)*
12 past tense of lead *(3)*
13 verb meaning to build *(5)*
15 past tense of 8 across *(4)*
18 I ____ do it tomorrow *(4)*
19 tailless monkey, verb meaning to imitate *(3)*
21 past tense of sing *(4)*
22 present tense of dented *(4)*
23 present tense of fried *(3)*
25 knock gently *(3)*
27 confused comment *(2)*
28 present tense of did *(2)*

## Marco Polo

Marco Polo was a Venetian. His family were merchants in Venice, in Italy. In about 1260, when Marco was seven, his father, Nicolo, and his uncle, Maffeo, made a long and dangerous journey to China. China was then called Cathay and Europeans knew almost nothing about lands so far east. In Cathay they met Kublai Khan, the ruler of that part of Asia. They came back safely in 1271, and then decided to return to Cathay, this time taking Marco with them.

The reason for their journey was trade. The merchants of Italy were eager to open up safe routes and control the trade between the East and the rest of Europe. Demand for the silks and spices of the East was great and there was a chance to make a lot of money.

In 1271 they sailed from Venice to Acre and then went overland to Hormuz, at the mouth of the Arabian Gulf. They wanted to take a ship from Hormuz, but changed their minds and went north-east across Persia. Then they travelled over the high mountains and down to the Gobi Desert. They crossed the desert and made for Shangtu, the summer capital of Cathay. They arrived early in 1275 after a very long and often dangerous journey.

They were welcomed here by Kublai Khan. Marco studied the language and became a sort of ambassador. He travelled all over Asia in the service of the Khan for more than thirteen years. Eventually, in 1290, he and his crew sailed for home. The sea journey back to Hormuz took two years because of delays in Sumatra and South India. From there, they went overland to Trebizond and then sailed back to Venice, arriving in 1295. They had been away for twenty-four years.

In Venice, nobody believed their stories of strange lands, peoples and customs and Marco became famous for telling hundreds of "tall" stories. However, their riches and the things they brought back spoke for them, and people began to believe what they said. Marco wrote about his travels, describing strange people, animals and lands such as Tibet, Burma, Laos, Japan, Madagascar and Sumatra. Because of Marco Polo, interest in and trade with the East increased. He never left Venice again and died in 1324. War later closed Marco's route for two hundred years and Europeans had to find another way to the East.

Answer the following questions using one sentence for each question. Do not number your sentences, let them follow each other to make a paragraph. Indent your paragraph.

1 When and where was Marco Polo born? (*begin* Marco Polo was . . .)
2 What did his father do? (*begin* His father . . .)
3 Where had his father been?
4 Why did they want to go to Cathay again?
5 When did Marco's journey begin?
6 What route did he take?
7 How long did the journey take?
8 Was it an easy journey?
9 Who was Kublai Khan?
10 What did Marco do in Cathay?
11 How long did he stay?
12 When did he return?
13 How long had he been away from Venice?
14 What happened when he reached home?
15 What did people learn from Marco's experiences?
16 When did he die?

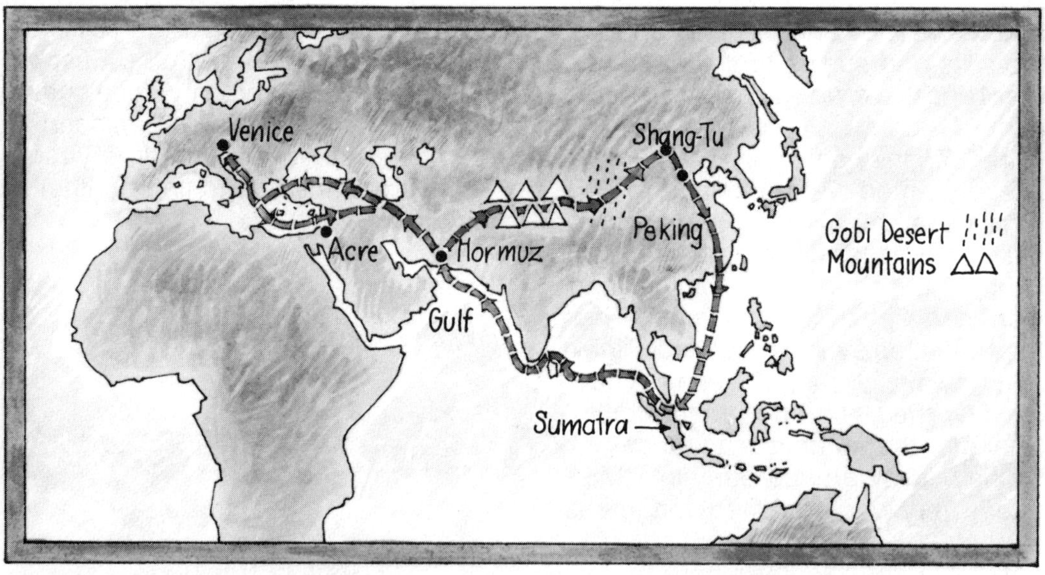


**Dictionary Exercise**

Use each of these words in a sentence so that its meaning is clear:

| | | | | |
|---|---|---|---|---|
| 1 sensible | 2 timid | 3 shy | 4 silent | 5 fruity |
| 6 depressed | 7 sneaky | 8 brutal | 9 graceful | 10 unhealthy |
| 11 shallow | 12 steep | 13 unpopular | 14 mean | 15 unfriendly |
| 16 unpleasant | 17 unattractive | 18 powerful | 19 expensive | 20 careless |

# Adjectives

**Adjectives** are describing words.
For example, happy, huge, hairy, heavy, honest, high, horrible.

**A** Adjectives describe people, places or things.
A noun is the name of a person, place or thing.
Therefore adjectives describe nouns.

| **adjective** | **noun** | |
|---|---|---|
| sharp | knife | = a sharp knife |
| shabby | coat | = a shabby coat |
| small | boy | = a small boy |
| smelly | sock | = a smelly sock |
| sad | story | = a sad story |
| silly | mistake | = a silly mistake |

In the next two sentences the adjectives have been underlined.

The young singer made a magnificent debut. The delighted audience enjoyed an entertaining evening of exhilarating music.

Obviously a pleasant evening was enjoyed by all – but if we remove the adjectives from the account of the concert we are left with:

The singer made a debut. The audience enjoyed an evening of music.

This does not tell us much about the success of the concert.

**B** Adjectives are used to give a fuller, more descriptive and accurate account of people, places, things and events.
The adjectives have been underlined in the next sentence.

Skilful, adventurous Sam Smith scored a remarkable goal in front of the 25,000 admiring supporters at Brick United's tiny East London football ground on Saturday.

Without the adjectives, we know nothing of Sam Smith, the supporters or the ground. We do not even know which side Sam is on:

Sam Smith scored a goal in front of the supporters at Brick United's ground on Saturday.

**Exercise 1**
Select adjectives from the brackets to add meaning to each of the following sentences:

**1** Saturday was a (wet, windy, foggy, chilly, bright) day.
**2** Science is my (favourite, worst, strongest, weakest) subject.
**3** That girl is a (quick, intelligent, unpleasant, dull) student.
**4** Pick up that (disgusting, filthy, valuable, scruffy) book!
**5** My mother is a (considerate, youthful, interesting, sensible) lady.
**6** That child is a (cruel, dishonest, unattractive, rude) boy.
**7** The (tall, lanky, slim) gentleman wore a (blue, old, shabby) coat.
**8** John is a (friendly, tidy, rude) boy with (fussy, generous) parents.
**9** We drank some (revolting, strong, hot, tepid) tea.
**10** The weather was (cloudless, stormy, sunny, wet) yesterday.

**C** There are many alternative ways of describing similar features.

Even very ordinary objects may be described so that they can be told apart from other similar objects.

**Exercise 2**
Write down as many adjectives as you can think of to describe:

**1** a bus
**2** a dustbin
**3** your school
**4** the weather today
**5** your exercise book

Try to present your answers in the diagramatic form shown here.

# Alphabetical Order Revision

**Exercise 1**

Place these fruits in alphabetical order:
plum grape peach grapefruit raspberry
pear apricot prune raisin gooseberry.

**Exercise 2**

Place these vegetables in alphabetical order:
cucumber radish spinach cabbage celery
sprout potato broccoli pea swede.

**Exercise 3**

Place these edible fish in alphabetical order:
salmon haddock sardine hake skate
shrimp halibut sole scampi herring.

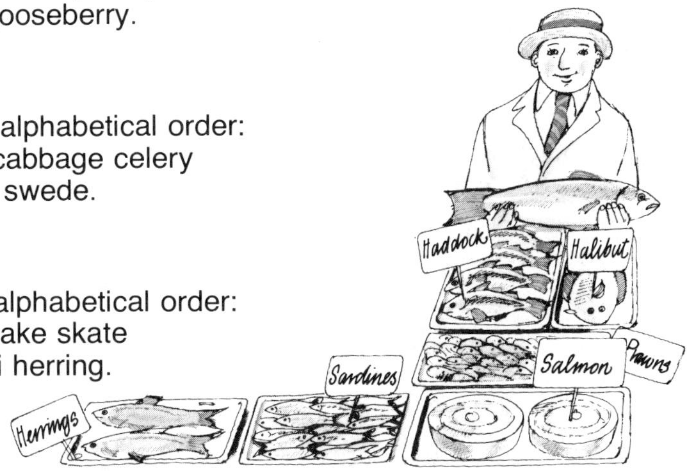


**A** When two or more people have the same **surname,** for example in a form register, you put them in alphabetical order by looking at their **initials**.

**Example 1**

| | | |
|---|---|---|
| **J**.R. Smith | The surnames are | A.L. Smith |
| **P**.T. Smith | the same, so look | J.R. Smith |
| **A**.L. Smith | at the first initials – | P.T. Smith |
| | **J. P. A.** | |
| | Put these in alphabetical order | |

**Example 2**

| | | |
|---|---|---|
| S.**P**. Singh | The surnames are the same. | S.B. Singh |
| S.**M**. Singh | The **first** initials are the same. | S.M. Singh |
| S.**B**. Singh | Look at the **second** initials – | S.P. Singh |
| | P. M. B. | |
| | Put these in alphabetical order | |

**Exercise 1**

Arrange the Green family in alphabetical order:
P.L. Green W.B. Green C.G. Green H.S. Green M.P. Green

**Exercise 2**

Arrange the following names in alphabetical order:
C.H. Carter C.C. Carter C.D. Carter C.V. Carter C.A. Carter

**Exercise 3**

Look carefully at the names below. Sort them into **surname** groups first, then look at their **initials** and arrange all the names in alphabetical order.

| | | |
|---|---|---|
| M.V. Winter | B.M. Wind | M.L. Winter |
| C.D. Wind | M.A. Winter | L.T. Wine |
| M.M. Wine | L.V. Wine | B.P. Wind |

**Exercise 4**

Look at the page from the telephone directory opposite, and see if you can answer the following questions:

**1** What is the telephone number of:
**a)** R.A. Snow **b)** J.O. Soane **c)** M.R. Snowden **d)** J.G. Soane

**2** What is the address of:
**a)** D.J. Snow **b)** E.A. Snowdon **c)** N.A. Snowie **d)** R.R. Snow

**3** What is the telephone number of:
**a)** S. Snowdon, 105a Moyser Road, S.W.16
**b)** M.E. Snowden, 2 Cumberland Road, W.7
**c)** N. Snow, 14 Shirehall Lane, N.W.4

**4** Why do all the numbers begin with 01?

**5** Find a pair of names that sound the same but are spelt differently.

**6** Get your local telephone directory and look through the first few pages. Find the numbers to ring for the following information:
**a)** the time
**b)** Directory Enquiries
**c)** the Test Match score
**d)** the weather forecast for Liverpool
**e)** motoring information for Manchester

**B** You will have noticed many **abbreviations** or shortened forms by now. For example, Rd. is used instead of Road. This saves space and money.

**7** Can you write the following abbreviations out in full:
Av. St. Gdns. Sq. Ho. Clo. Cres. La. Gro. Pk. Ct.

**8** Now work out these two examples of abbreviations used for occupations. What do the following do for a living:
**a)** John Snow **b)** J. Snowdon of St. James Street.

Snow D.A.D, 19 Mountjoy Clo SE2 .....01- 4002
Snow D.C, 45 Wilton Gro SW19 .....01- 6017
Snow D.H, 66a Alexandra Pk Rd N10 .....01- 0703
Snow D.J, 68 Harvey Gdns SE7 .....01- 0542
Snow D.P, 2 Firs La N21 .....01- 8793
Snow D.S, 181 Russell Av N22 .....01- 3734
Snow D.W, 45 St. Olaves Est,Druid St SE1 .....01- 0550
Snow E, 4 Boscombe Rd SW17 .....01- 5413
Snow E, 6 Allen Ho,Suffolk Rd SE25 .....01- 4730
Snow E.H.W, 22b St. Swithins Rd SE13 .....01- 2272
Snow Ernest L, 78 High Gro SE18 .....01- 1634
Snow E.T, 3 Braeside Rd SW16 .....01- 5488
Snow F, 53 Witherington Rd N5 .....01- 2397
Snow F.A, 148 Priory Ct,South Countess Rd E17 .....01- 4312
Snow F.A, 4 Vaughan Av W6 .....01- 8946
Snow F.J.A, 5 St.Margarets Gro SE18 .....01- 5797
**SNOW SIR FREDERICK & PARTNERS,Conslt Engs— Ross Ho, Southwark St SE1** .....01- 5688
Snow F.R, 6 Leonard Rd E7 .....01- 5689
Snow G, 46 Winford Ho,Jodrell Rd E3 .....01- 3074
Snow G, 11 Sacksville Ho,Myddleton Rd N8 .....01- 2204
Snow G, 1 St. Andrews Rd W14 .....01- 1907
Snow George, 1 St. Andrews Rd W14 .....01- 4112
Snow G.H, 36 Granham Gdns N9 .....01- 2455
Snow H.D, 5 The Gables,Vale of Health NW3 .....01- 8557
Snow H.H, 62 Leyborne Av W13 .....01- 2127
Snow H.M, 132 Mallinson Rd SW11 .....01- 2016
Snow H.R, 11 Bassein Pk Rd W12 .....01- 5979
Snow Ian, 156 Southwark Bdge Rd SE1 .....01- 1762
Snow J, 106 Corporation St E15 .....01- 0433
Snow John,Nwsagt, 378 Uxbridge Rd W12 .....01- 4640
Snow J.A, 338 Long La N2 .....01- 3524
Snow J.B, 62 Springfield Rd E17 .....01- 8675
Snow J.E, 84 Wellington Gdns SE7 .....01- 5487
Snow J.F, 14 St. Albans Av E6 .....01- 2166
Snow J.F.R, 5 Hurst Clo E4 .....01- 1646
Snow John R,Elec Contr, 34 Lowell St E14 .....01- 3833
Snow J.R, 68 Carradale Ho,St. Leonards Rd E14 .....01- 3833
Snow K, 221 Vivian Ct,Maida Va W9 .....01- 4402
Snow Kitty, 1 Shelley Ho,Roman Rd E2 .....01- 4745
Snow K, 32 Wrens Pk Ho,Warwick Gro E5 .....01- 2295
Snow K.R, 178 Mitcham Rd E6 .....01- 2413
Snow Leonard, 15 Halstow Rd SE10 .....01- 4257
Snow L.F, 55 Ainslie Wd Gdns E4 .....01- 4918
Snow L.G, 35 Huxley Rd E10 .....01- 7214
Snow L.M.C, 127 Hambalt Rd SW4 .....01- 2603
Snow L.R.C, 28 Bercta Rd SE9 .....01- 4533
Snow M, 13s Peabody Bldgs Chequer St EC1 .....01- 0428
Snow Michael, 4 Horder Rd SW6 .....01- 3819
Snow M.C, 17 Lower Hall La E4 .....01- 2314
Snow M.D, 20 Spalding Ho,Honor Oak Est SE4 .....01- 6603
Snow M.F, 31 Clifton Ct,Studholme St SE15 .....01- 9809
Snow M.J, 8 Glenwood Av NW9 .....01- 4310
Snow M.P, 4 Second Av E12 .....01- 5274
Snow N, 4a Queens Rd SE15 .....01- 1782
Snow N, 14 Shirehall La NW4 .....01- 7395
Snow N.A.W, 12 Culworth Ho,Allitsen Rd NW8 .....01- 7244
Snow N.E, 78 Delaware Mans,Delaware Rd W9 .....01- 1766
Snow N.Fenn,Chrpdst, 494 Harrow Rd W9 .....01- 1493
Snow N.F, 10 Hawthorne Gro NW9 .....01- 8071
Snow P, 20 Preston Ho,Abbey St SE1 .....01- 8406
Snow Peter, 4 Ashness Rd SW11 .....01- 2505
Snow Peter, 98 Sherbourne Ct,Cromwell Rd SW5 .....01- 8998
Snow P, 55 Nobel Ho,Flaxman Rd SE5 .....01- 5948
Snow P, 4 Drew Av,Inglis Barracks NW7 .....01- 4814
Snow P.B, 15 Faraday Mans,Queens Clb Gdns W14 .....01- 7778
Snow P.F, 131 Kennington Pk Rd SE11 .....01- 6599
Snow P.L, 3 Bebbington Rd SE18 .....01- 9620
Snow P.N, 11/43 Ponder St N7 .....01- 7138
Snow P.R, 73 Peabody Twrs,Golden La EC1 .....01- 3338
Snow Robert, 18 Bagleys Ln SW6 .....01- 6093
Snow Reginald, 5 Charles Grinling Wlk SE18 .....01- 6562
Snow R.A, 1 Willrose Cres SE2 .....01- 5372
Snow R.E, 28 Lockhart Clo N7 .....01- 1144
Snow R.E.A, 217 Cavendish Av W13 .....01- 4779
Snow R.G.& Co.Ltd, 139 Tooley St SE1 .....01- 5802
Snow Robt.H, 267 Wricklemarsh Rd SE3 .....01- 0668
Snow R.J, 4 Sherborne Gdns W13 .....01- 4425
Snow R.M, 107 John Ruskin St SE5 .....01- 3392
Snow R.R, 22 Chelwood,Oakleigh Rd Nth N20 .....01- 5382
Snow R.W, 55 Blaney Cres E6 .....01- 0467
Snow R.W, 23 The Grange SW19 .....01- 2891
Do. .....01- 7121
Snow S, 70 Coverack Clo N14 .....01- 0380

**SNOWCREST Ltd,Ice Cr Mfrs, 8 Whites Rw E1** .....01- 5525
Snowden A.C, 41 Godfrey St SW3 .....01- 6756
Snowden B.D, 6 Trojan Ct,Grosvenor Rd W7 .....01- 3105
Snowden Mrs B.I, 5 Jenkins Ho,Thessaly Rd SW8 .....01- 5744
Snowden D.S, 5 Ewald Rd SW6 .....01- 5480
Snowden E, 4 Edward Friend Ho,Brodia Rd N16 .....01- 8489
Snowden E, 187 The Vale NW11 .....01- 6795
Snowden E.L, 281 Ilderton Rd SE15 .....01- 9315
Snowden F.A, 5 Folkington Cnr N12 .....01- 7607
Snowden G.F, 46 De Vere Gdns W8 .....01- 0510
Snowden H.G, 6 Pekin St E14 .....01- 4987
Snowden Ivor, 20 Cambridge Mans,Cambridge Rd SW11 .....01- 5208
Snowden Ian, 10 Chaldon Rd SW6 .....01- 1727
Snowden J.A, 24 Pullman Ct,Streatham Hl SW2 .....01- 3477
Snowden J.A.K, 34 Hollingbourne Rd SE24 .....01- 1780
Snowden J.F, 19 Oakman Ho,Tilford Gdns SW19 .....01- 2214
Snowden J.L, 46 Midmoor Rd SW12 .....01- 2580
Snowden M, 62a Cranhurst Rd NW2 .....01- 2340
Snowden M.E, 25 John Trundle Ct,Barbican EC2 .....01- 5357
Snowden M.E, 2 Cumberland Rd W7 .....01- 0575
Snowden M.R, 3 Holly Village N6 .....01- 7121
Snowden R, 10 Knoll Ct,Farquhar Rd SE19 .....01- 1177
Snowden R.L, 2 Trewint St SW18 .....01- 5732
Snowden Raymond W, 170 Cranmer Ct,Sloane Av SW3 .....01- 4317
Snowden V.J, 32 Rectory Rd E17 .....01- 0370
Snowdex Ltd,Filing System Mfrs, 99 Crawford St W1 .....01- 0741
Snowdin M.D, 15 Hambrook Rd SE25 .....01- 3810
Snowdon A, 64 Chatham Rd E17 .....01- 9023
Snowdon A, 20 South Va SE19 .....01- 2608
Snowdon Arthur J, 17 Belgrave Rd E10 .....01- 4075
Snowdon Arthur J,Furn, 157b Mare St E8 .....01- 6757
Snowdon B, 53 Woodville Gdns W5 .....01- 3354
Snowdon Dr B.A, 25 Knollys Rd SW16 .....01- 1424
Snowdon B.J, 2/13 Elm Gro Rd W5 .....01- 1634
Snowdon C.W, 62 Dowanhill Rd SE6 .....01- 5670
Snowdon E, 115 Brook La SE3 .....01- 1256
Snowdon E.A, 104 Verdun Rd SW13 .....01- 3294
Snowdon E.C, 58 Fairlight Av E4 .....01- 1528
Snowdon G.F, 28 Clinch Ct,Plymouth Rd E16 .....01- 4699
Snowdon H.A, 5 De Beauvoir Sq N1 .....01- 6743
Snowdon I, 9 Samels Ct,South Black Lion La W6 .....01- 0832
Snowdon I.B, 133 Tooting High St SW17 .....01- 1703
Snowdon J, 11 Ormond Rd N19 .....01- 0597
Snowdon J,Furn Mfrs, 74 St. James St E17 .....01- 3429
Snowdon J.H, 124 Walpole Rd E18 .....01- 0565
Snowdon J.K, 9 Station Ct,Gibbon Rd SE15 .....01- 2732
Snowdon J.M, 18 Carol St NW1 .....01- 7191
Snowdon K.J, 8 Horsmonden Rd SE4 .....01- 5426
Snowdon Leslie, 49 Whitby Ct,Parkhurst Rd N7 .....01- 4479
Snowdon M.E, 167 Hazelbank Rd SE6 .....01- 3336
Snowdon Mountain Railway Ltd, 3 Catherine Pl SW1 .....01- 1462
Snowdon N.M, 98 Scott Ellis Gdns NW8 .....01- 1599
Snowdon R, 15 Copeland Ho,Garratt La SW17 .....01- 4603
Snowdon Raymnd G, 51 Morpeth St E2 .....01- 4392
Snowdon R.J, 19 Belgrave Rd E10 .....01- 7217
Snowdon Roger Presentations, 14a Old Compton St W1 .....01- 1850
Snowdon S, 22 Burghley Rd E11 .....01- 0587
Snowdon S, 105a Moyser Rd SW16 .....01- 3851
Snowdonia Bedding Ltd, 96 Leonard St EC2 .....01- 3082
Do. .....01- 3811
Snowdons Car Hire Service, 35 Boundary Rd E13 .....01- 2757
Snowdown E.F, 2 Albert Rd E18 .....01- 2817
Snowie N.A, 53 Boileau Rd W5 .....01- 3850
Snowland Leather Fashion Co,Mfrs Lthr Garments, 94 Middlesex St E1 .....01- 8544
Soan V, 324 Acton Mws E8 .....01- 7270
Soan V, 43 St. Paul St N1 .....01- 4710
Soan W, 51 Henningham Rd N17 .....01- 6680
Soane A.J, 28 Mount Rd SW19 .....01- 0757
Soane C.D, 174 Golders Gn Rd NW11 .....01- 9691
Soane J.G, 3 Thorpe Rd E17 .....01- 3219
Soane J.O, 140a Tanfield Av NW2 .....01- 8223
Soane L, 1 Newton Ho,Union Gro SW8 .....01- 2384
Soane R.J, 22 Monmouth Rd E6 .....01- 2487
Soane T, 10 Alderville Rd SW6 .....01- 6069
Soane W.G.A, 2 Richmond Vill,Chingford Rd E17 .....01- 3449
Soanes B.E, 3 Wellstead Av N9 .....01- 1583
Soanes C.T, 39 Rayne Ct E18 .....01- 2455
Soanes Capt D.R, 89 Mayday Gdns SE3 .....01- 7791
Soanes E, 5/320 Earls Ct Rd SW5 .....01- 9942

# The Apostrophe (1)

An apostrophe is a comma placed above the letters in a word.
It is used in this section to show that one or more letters has been left out of a word.

For example, do n**o**t becomes don't – the second **o** has been left out. An apostrophe takes its place.

I **a**m becomes I'm – the **a** has been left out. The apostrophe is where the **a** had been.

**Exercise 1**
In this exercise you must write out the words in full. One letter has been replaced by an apostrophe.

**1** I'm **2** he's **3** couldn't **4** shouldn't **5** don't
**6** she's **7** didn't **8** isn't **9** wasn't **10** mustn't

**Exercise 2**
By replacing **one** letter by an apostrophe shorten these words.

**1** what is **2** there is **3** who is **4** where is **5** here is
**6** are not **7** were not **8** has not **9** they are **10** we are

**A** Sometimes two letters are replaced by **one** apostrophe.
For example, can**no**t becomes can't – the second **n** and the **o** are replaced by one apostrophe.

**Exercise 3**
Write out in full these shortened words. In each example, two letters have been replaced by one apostrophe.

**1** I'll **2** you'll **3** he'll **4** she'll **5** they'll
**6** we'll **7** can't **8** could've **9** I've **10** you've

**Exercise 4**
Use one apostrophe to shorten these words. In each case two letters are to be replaced by the apostrophe.

**1** it will **2** they have **3** would have **4** should have **5** we have
**6** you have **7** she will **8** I will **9** could have **10** might have

**B** Sometimes more than two letters are left out. Again, we use only **one** apostrophe.

| | | | |
|---|---|---|---|
| For example, | I **woul**d be happy to come | becomes | I'd be happy to come. |

Four letters are replaced by one apostrophe.

| | | | |
|---|---|---|---|
| For example, | He **woul**d like to go home | becomes | He'd like to go home. |

Again, four letters are replaced by one apostrophe.

**Other examples:**

ne**v**er becomes ne'er
e**v**er becomes e'er } mainly in old poetry
7 o**f the** clock becomes 7 o'clock
**i**t is becomes 'tis
So**uthamp**ton becomes So'ton
B**irming**ham becomes B'ham } often in football results

**C** The shortened versions of words should **only** be used when you are writing what a person **said**.

For example, "Don't jump!" he shouted.
"I can't do this work," he said.
"What's the time?" she asked.

# Christopher Columbus

Christopher Columbus was born in Genoa, in Italy, in 1451. He was the son of a weaver. Not much is known about his early life, but we do know that he was a sailor, and that he was ship-wrecked and landed in Portugal, where he stayed.

Columbus went to the Canary Islands, and there began to form his idea of reaching India by sailing west instead of east. It was a long way to India from the east, but if the world was round, as he thought, it would be a much shorter distance going from the other direction.

Columbus presented his idea to the King of Portugal, but it was rejected. He then went to Spain, and spent six years persuading people to support him with money. Finally, on August 3rd 1492, he set sail with three ships, the Santa Maria, the Pinta and the Nina. He reached the Canary Islands first and then set out across the Atlantic Ocean.

The sailors became bored and also frightened during the long journey, but on October 12th, they sighted land. This land was not an island off the east coast of India, as they expected, but San Salvador, an island in the Bahamas off the east coast of America. No one in Europe knew America existed then; the Vikings had reached it much earlier, but this had long been forgotten.

Columbus sailed round various islands in search of gold. He set up a small colony and took some slaves. Finally he came back to Spain in January 1493, where he was greatly honoured and given land and wealth.

Columbus went back to the "New World" three times, discovering more and more islands. Gradually, more and more people went out also, towns were built and the Spanish Government took control of lands that Columbus thought of as his own.

He died in Spain in 1506. His original plan of going west to reach India was soon to be completed by another discoverer.

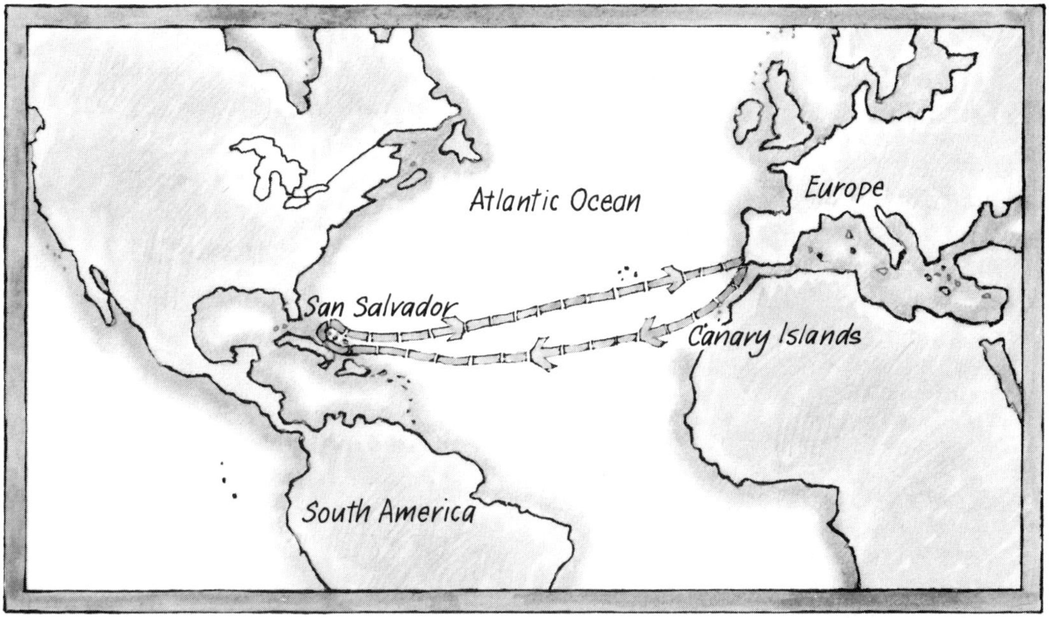


When you have read the previous passage about Columbus and looked at the map, write out the **questions** that would be asked to give the answers below.
For example, **answer:** 1451 **question:** When was Christopher Columbus born?

**1** In Genoa in Italy.
**2** He wanted to find a new route to India.
**3** The King of Portugal.
**4** Six years.
**5** August 3rd 1492.
**6** The Santa Maria, the Nina and the Pinta.
**7** The Canary Islands.
**8** October 12th 1492.
**9** San Salvador.
**10** The Vikings.
**11** In January 1493.
**12** He was honoured and given land and wealth.
**13** Three times.
**14** 1506, in Spain.

**Dictionary Exercise**
Use each of the following words in a sentence so that its meaning is clear:

**1** admire **2** magnificent **3** exhilarating **4** adventurous **5** attractive
**6** delicate **7** generous **8** brutal **9** slender **10** petty

# Letter-Writing

## A Business or Official Letters

Your address, so people know where to contact you when they reply.

27 Rotten Street,
Grease Park,
London, E.12.

Notice the position of the commas and full stop.

23rd November 1981

Always write the date.

The address of the person or firm you are writing to.

Note the use of commas and full stop.

Funny Toys Ltd,
66 Empty Rd,
Mudtown.

If you know the name of the person you are writing to, use it. For example, Dear Mrs. Smith

Dear Sirs,

We always begin the letter underneath the comma.

Last Friday I bought one of the Silly Mouse toys from your Mudtown store. When I got it home I noticed that the toy's head was held in place by an elastic band which subsequently snapped. The toy's head fell off and was followed by three of its four legs.

I am enclosing the remains of my Silly Mouse and expect to receive a refund of the £1.27 I paid for the toy. I am sure you will agree that a headless, one-legged mouse looks very silly indeed.

Content of the letter.

If you know the name of the person you are writing to, end the letter, Yours sincerely

Yours faithfully,

Mr I. Amangry

Your signature, so the reader knows who is writing.

**Exercise 1**
Imagine that you are the manager of Funny Toys Ltd and that you do not wish to refund I. Amangry's £1.27. Write a letter to Mr. Amangry explaining your position. Remember, you know his name so you should end your letter, "Yours sincerely". Lay out your letter as shown above.

**Exercise 2**

This is the sort of letter often appearing in local newspapers.

> Mump Cottage,
> Nice Place Avenue,
> Treetown.
> 23rd November 1981.
>
> The Editor,
> Daily Dot,
> News Road,
> Treetown.
>
> Dear Sir,
>
> I feel I must write to you concerning the attitudes of todays youngsters. After visiting my grandchildren I have come to the opinion that children spend all their time watching television and lazing around. They never seem to read books anymore and hardly know what a newspaper looks like. Where's it all going to end?
>
> Yours faithfully,
> Gladys Snodney (Mrs)

Reply to Mrs. Snodney's letter using the results of the questionnaire below.

The results of a class questionnaire on the reading and television viewing of a first-year form in Bidley Comprehensive School

| QUESTIONS | POSSIBLE ANSWERS | NUMBERS REPLYING | AVERAGE PER PUPIL |
|---|---|---|---|
| 1) How many hours a night do you spend watching television? | a) under 1 hour | 4 | |
| | b) 1–2 hours | 17 | 2 hours |
| | c) 2–4 hours | 9 | |
| | d) over 4 hours | 0 | |
| 2) How much time do you spend on homework each night? | a) under 1 hour | 10 | |
| | b) 1–2 hours | 14 | $1\frac{1}{2}$ hours |
| | c) over 2 hours | 6 | |
| 3) Do you regularly read a newspaper? | a) yes | 16 | |
| | b) no | 14 | |
| 4) How many books have you read in the last month? | a) none | 3 | |
| | b) one | 11 | 2 books |
| | c) two to four | 13 | |
| | d) over four | 3 | |

**B Letters to a Friend or Relative**

When writing to someone with whom you are on friendly terms, the basic form of the letter is the same as for business letters. But:

1 You write "Dear Sally," or "Dear Uncle Bill," rather than using "Dear Madam," or "Dear Sir".
2 You do not need to write their address on your letter.
3 You use less formal English. Letters to friends are often chatty, business letters are concise and formal.
4 You can end your letter with "Yours truly," "Love," "See you soon," or any other ending you may prefer.

25 Cabbage Avenue,
Tree Close,
Middlefield.
23rd November 1981.

Dear Ivy,

Thanks for your letter inviting me to stay at your house this weekend. I'd love to come and my parents say it is all right as long as I come home by Sunday afternoon to finish my homework. I will arrive at Central Station at 11·00 a.m. on Saturday. I hope you can meet me there.

Love
Claudette.

**C Addressing the Envelope**

William Morris
942 Slops Road
Little Haven
S. Yorks.

The most important thing about the envelope is that people in the Post Office must be able to read it.

Remember to leave space for the postage stamp.

The usual form for addressing envelopes is shown here.

**Exercise 3**

Write a letter to a friend who has moved away from your area. Describe your secondary school to him or her. Beneath the letter, address an envelope.

# Opposites

Opposites are two words that are totally different in meaning.
For example, good is the opposite of bad, happy is the opposite of sad, clean is the opposite of dirty, dropped is the opposite of caught.

**Exercise 1**
Match each word in the left-hand box with its opposite in the right-hand box.

| | |
|---|---|
| **1** hot | **2** north |
| **3** cool | **4** dawn |
| **5** east | **6** left |
| **7** barren | **8** sunrise |
| **9** shallow | **10** smooth |

| | |
|---|---|
| dusk | warm |
| fertile | south |
| cold | rough |
| sunset | right |
| deep | west |

**Exercise 2**
Find a verb opposite in meaning to the following verbs:

| | | | | |
|---|---|---|---|---|
| **1** start | **2** shout | **3** fail | **4** rise | **5** go |
| **6** forget | **7** find | **8** arrive | **9** warm | **10** catch |

**Exercise 3**
Find an adjective opposite in meaning to these adjectives:

| | | | | |
|---|---|---|---|---|
| **1** sad | **2** dirty | **3** white | **4** correct | **5** tall |
| **6** fat | **7** enormous | **8** quiet | **9** old | **10** ancient |

**Exercise 4**
Find a noun opposite in meaning to each of these nouns:

| | | | | |
|---|---|---|---|---|
| **1** sadness | **2** adult | **3** slavery | **4** daytime | **5** afternoon |
| **6** love | **7** front | **8** end | **9** evil | **10** background |

**A** Some words form their opposites by fixing extra letters at their beginning. These extra letters are called a **prefix**.
For example, legal – illegal, correct – incorrect, well – unwell.

**Exercise 5**
Find the opposite of each of these words. In numbers 1 to 5, a prefix is required to form the opposite. In numbers 6–10, the prefix must be removed to find the opposite.
When you have found the opposite of each word use it in a sentence so that its meaning is clear.

| | | | | |
|---|---|---|---|---|
| **1** tied | **2** kind | **3** lucky | **4** perfect | **5** clear |
| **6** irregular | **7** incompetent | **8** impossible | **9** unlikely | **10** insoluble |

# Revision (1)

**Exercise 1**
**Sentences Practice**
This paragraph deals with the Hindu religion. Copy out the passage and put in the capital letters and full stops so that it is written in nine sentences.

Most people in India are Hindus over 300 million people practise the Hindu religion the Hindus worship many gods and have many images of them these gods are different ways of speaking about one god this spirit is called Brahman prayer is performed alone there are few great festivals where people worship together there are many holy books the three most important ones are the Vedas, Upanishads and Gita.

**Exercise 2**
**Singular and Plural Revision**
The following passage mixes a singular description of **a mammal** with a plural description of **mammals**. Separate it into two separate paragraphs, one singular and one plural. Write them out.
The underlined words must go in **both** paragraphs.
For example, **1** A mammal is .....
**2** Mammals are .....

A mammal mammals is are a vertebrate animal animals, meaning it they has have a backbone. A mammal mammals is are usually covered with hair, wool or fur. It they is are warm-blooded. A mammal mammals do does not lay eggs, it they give gives birth to live young. It they feed feeds its their young with milk. Mammals a mammal that eat eats meat is are called a carnivore carnivores. A mammal mammals that eat eats plants is are called a herbivore herbivores. Mammals a mammal that eats eat plants and meat is are called an omnivore omnivores.

**Exercise 3**
**Opposites Revision**
In the box on the right there are twenty pairs of opposites for you to match up. Write them out in pairs.

accept increase lengthen decrease pleasure
honest deep west enemy victory sadness defend
yes purchase ally shorten refuse hinder sell pain
defeat honesty shallow east dishonesty dishonest
happiness attack contract no help expand infertile
freeze fertile impossible cool thaw possible warm.

# The South Pole

In 1911 Roald Amundsen and Captain R. Scott both led expeditions to reach the South Pole. The map shows the different routes they took.

The following passage contains sentences about both expeditions together. Divide the passage into two separate paragraphs, one dealing with Amundsen and one with Scott.
Remember to indent each paragraph.

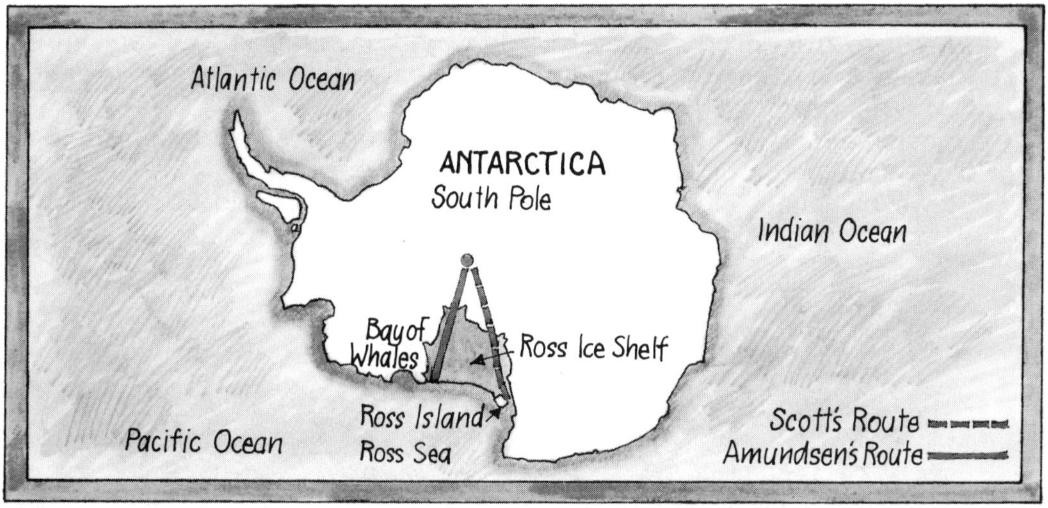


In 1910 Captain R. Scott left England in the ship Terra Nova. He sailed to Antarctica to investigate the Ross Sea area and to try to reach the South Pole. In 1910 Roald Amundsen sailed from Norway to Antarctica in the ship Fram. He had intended to go to the North Pole but someone else had got there first, so he decided to try for the South Pole. Scott's party set up a base on the west of Ross Island. Amundsen's party set up a base in the Bay of Whales on the Ross Ice Shelf. Amundsen set out with four companions on October 20th 1911. Scott set out with motor sledges, ponies and dogs. Amundsen took sledges and fifty-two dogs. He reached the South Pole on December 14th. Scott's motor-sledges soon broke down, the ponies were shot and later even the dog teams were sent back. Exhausted and pulling the sledges themselves, Scott's team reached the South Pole on January 17th 1912. Amundsen and his men returned safely in thirty-eight days and had twelve dogs left. Blizzards, exhaustion and a shortage of fuel finally beat Scott and his men. They died still a long way from their base. Their bodies were found on November 12th 1912.

# John and the Barons

Read the following passage carefully and then state which person, persons or object each underlined word refers to.
For example, line 1 his=Richard's.

After Richard's death, his brother John became King of England. He quarrelled with the King of France, and with the Pope. He also made enemies of many of his barons; they complained that he was hard and unfair because he gave heavy fines to any who displeased him and sometimes even seized their castles.

In the end, some of the barons joined together and rebelled against him. John agreed to meet them on the island of Runnymede in the Thames. There, in 1215, he agreed to a document called the Great Charter; this was written in Latin and called Magna Carta.

John agreed to rule the country according to the laws set down in the Great Charter and the barons promised to serve and obey him.

However, neither John nor the barons kept their promises for long and some of them continued to fight against him until the end of his reign.

**Dictionary Exercise**

Use each of these words in a sentence so that its meaning is clear:

**1** previous **2** swerve **3** accelerate **4** tease **5** regret
**6** satisfy **7** rely **8** imitate **9** relish **10** detest

# Revision (2)

## Exercise 1
## Sentences Practice

These three paragraphs on the Sikh religion have been written without punctuation. Copy out the passage and put in the full stops and capitals where they belong. The number of sentences in each paragraph is given in brackets.

there are over six million Sikhs in the world mostly living in the Punjab region of India where the Sikh religion began Sikh men are easily distinguished as they always have beards and wear turbans *(2)*

the sacred book of the Sikh religion is the Granth it is a collection of the teachings of a number of people the various teachings were brought together by Arjun he lived from 1563 until 1606 the Granth is written in Punjabi the Granth is composed of hymns these are set to music and chanted each day in the Sikh temples *(7)*

the Granth includes hymns by many Indian teachers most are Sikhs but there are also verses by Hindu and Moslem holy men there were ten great teachers of the Sikhs these masters are known as gurus after the tenth teacher died the Granth became the Sikh guru now it would guide them *(6)*

## Exercise 2
## Adjectives Revision

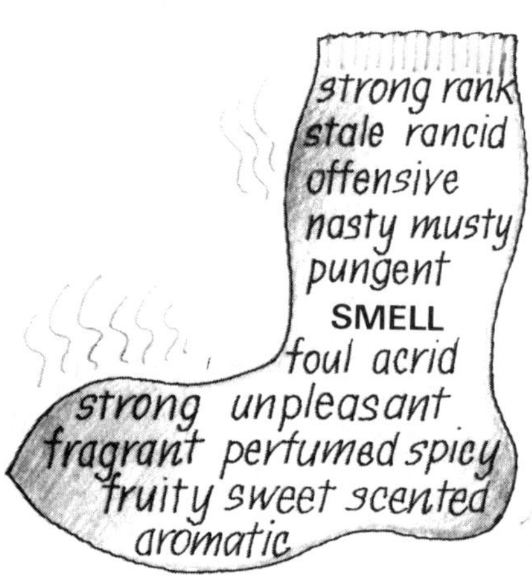

Write one paragraph on each of the following titles. Be sure to write descriptively, using appropriate adjectives. You may chose to use some of the adjectives above.

**1** A visit to the hospital

**2** School dinners

**3** The perfect holiday

**4** A day at the zoo

**Exercise 3**
Look at these shapes (you should know a lot of them already). The adjective that describes each shape is printed under it.

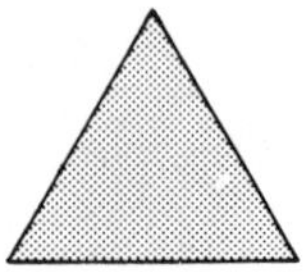
triangular

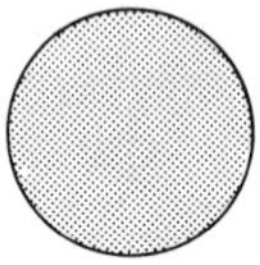
circular

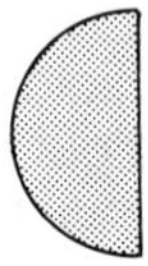
semi-circular

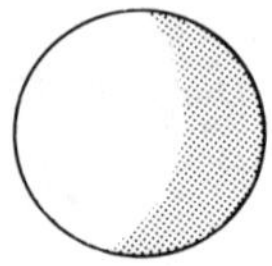
spherical

rectangular

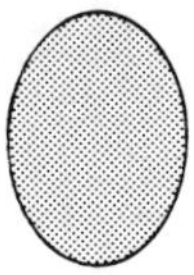
oval

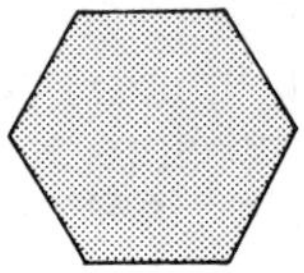
hexagonal

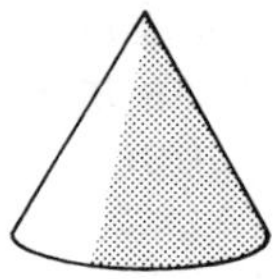
conical

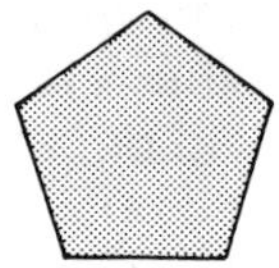
pentagonal

square

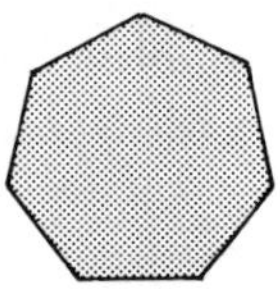
septagonal

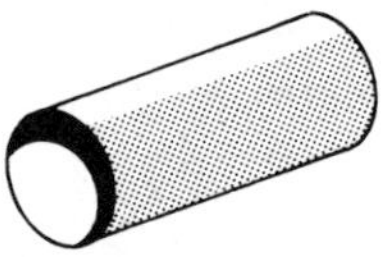
cylindrical

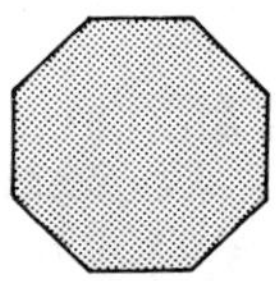
octagonal

**Exercise 4**
**Spelling Check**
Make a list of the adjectives above and write the nouns they come from beside them.
For example, circular – circle.

**Exercise 5**
Write out sentences describing the shape of the following objects.

For example, A five pound-note is rectangular.

# The Apostrophe (2)

A noun is the name of a person, place or thing.
For example, boy, woman, Mr. Smith, Eleni, school, room, zebra, box, cat.

**Exercise 1**

Copy out these sentences, and underline the nouns in them. Number 1 is done for you.

**1** The roof of Tony is leaking.
**2** The mother of Deborah is unhappy.
**3** The cat of Margaret is missing.
**4** The core of the apple is rotten.
**5** The bicycle of her father was stolen.
**6** The dog of Susan is trying to get out.
**7** The shop of Mrs. Jones is closed.
**8** I went to the house of Satnam.
**9** I found the dictionary of Eleni.
**10** The leaves of the tree are brown.

In each of these sentences one thing (a noun) belongs to another thing or person (a noun).
For example, The roof of Tony is leaking. (Roof and Tony are nouns.)
The roof belongs to Tony.

The bicycle of her father was stolen. (Bicycle and father are nouns.)
The bicycle belongs to her father.

The hat of the woman flew off. (Hat and woman are nouns.)
It is her hat, she owns it, it belongs to her.

We do not usually say:
The roof of Tony is leaking.
The bicycle of her father was stolen.
The hat of the woman flew off.
The shop of Mr. Smith is closed.

We usually say:
Tony's roof is leaking.
Her father's bicycle was stolen.
The woman's hat flew off.
Mr. Smith's shop is closed.

**A** To show that a thing **belongs to** someone we put **'s** at the end of the **owner's name**.
The thing owned comes straight after the owner.
For example, the man's car, Tony's roof, the woman's coat, the zebra's stripes, the teacher's desk, the book's cover, the cat's claws, Jane's pen.

**Exercise 2**
Put in the apostrophe where it belongs, rewriting the following sentences:

**1** Jims house burnt down last night.
**2** Janes house is being decorated.
**3** Kuldips mum has gone shopping.
**4** Manjits new book is torn already.
**5** I went to Clives house yesterday.
**6** I copied Laurels homework.
**7** Are you going to Elenis party?
**8** I had a lift to school in Lenas car.
**9** I like Harjeets new friend.
**10** Mandeeps work is very good.

**Exercise 3**
"The coat of the man" is a clumsy way of saying "The man's coat".
It uses too many words and looks strange. The following sentences are clumsy, so rewrite them, using the apostrophe to show that something belongs to someone.

**1** The owner of the dog could not save him from drowning.
**2** The temperature of the oven was far too hot.
**3** The nets of the fisherman were drying in the sun.
**4** The rays of the sun take several minutes to reach earth.
**5** The party of the girl was very enjoyable.
**6** The job of a policeman can be a pleasant one.
**7** That is the son of Mr. Singh over there.
**8** The claws of the tiger are sharp enough to kill.
**9** The expression on the face of the pilot was one of fear.
**10** The gloves of the boxer were torn and bloody.

**B** Often we wish to say that a thing **belongs to** a person even though it is **not owned** by that person.

| For example, | The pilot's face showed fear. | (The pilot does not own his face, but it **is** a part of him.) |
|---|---|---|
| | Mandeep's friend is very nice. | (The friend does not belong to Mandeep, but is **her** friend.) |
| | John's flat is well-heated. | (John rents his flat but considers it **his** flat.) |
| | Mary's mother has gone out. | (Mary never bought her mum, but she **is** Mary's mother.) |
| | The boy's birthday is on Monday. | (It is **his** birthday though he paid nothing for it.) |

**C** We can say that an apostrophe shows us that one noun belongs to, or is linked with, another noun.
Of course, a noun can be a thing as well as a person. A thing can **belong to** another thing.

For example, The book's cover was torn.
The hotel's bathrooms were dirty.
The toy's colour has faded.
The engine's drone was too loud.
The school's windows were smashed.

**This is Tony**

**Exercise 4**
Where do the arrows point on the drawing below? Begin each sentence, The arrow is pointing at . . .

**This is Marlene**

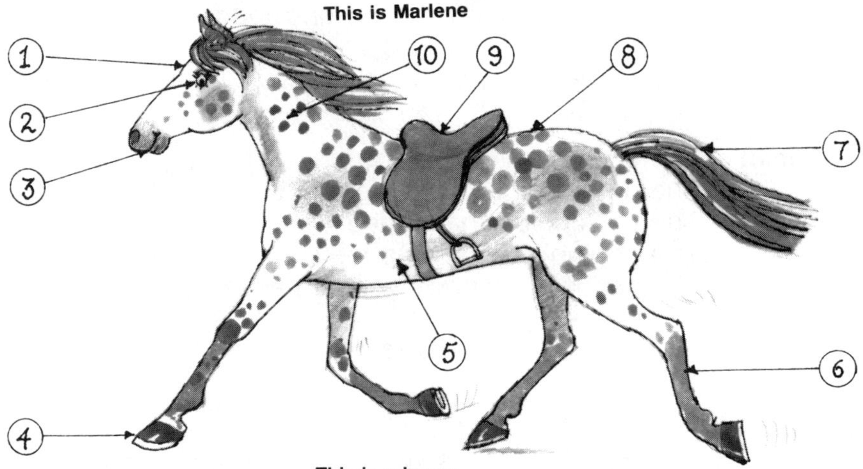


**This is a horse**

**D** We do **not** use an apostrophe every time we see an **s**.
We do **not** use an apostrophe when nothing belongs to a plural noun.
For example, Lloyd's friends are coming round tonight.

This means: the friends belonging to Lloyd are coming round tonight.
Therefore "Lloyd" has an apostrophe and **s**.
"Friends" has no apostrophe because nothing belongs to the friends.

Another example, The car's tyres are badly worn.
This means: the tyres belonging to the car are badly worn.
Therefore "car" has an apostrophe and **s**.
"Tyres" has an **s** because there are four tyres.
Nothing belongs to the tyres, so tyres has no apostrophe.

**Exercise 5**

Copy out these sentences and put in the apostrophes **only** where they belong:

**1** Lloyds friends got drunk last night.
**2** The cars tyres burst on the motorway.
**3** The horses legs are too tired to carry him on.
**4** The dogs eyes were closed as he was asleep.
**5** The leaves fall off our tree every Autumn.
**6** The tigers claws are through the net.
**7** My mothers sisters are visiting us.
**8** The teachers books fell on our desks.
**9** The books pages had been torn out by vandals.
**10** Johns clothes were all over the tables.

**E** So far we have looked at the use of apostrophes for singular nouns (one person, one place or one thing). Now we must look at plural nouns (more than one person, place or thing).
For example, boys, desks, thieves, churches, foxes, enemies, women.

If the owners are **plural** and **end in *s*** we show that they have something belonging to them by putting an apostrophe **after that *s***.
**We do not add another *s***.

**Some examples**

**1** "The books of the girl" becomes "The girl's books" (one owner)
**but**
**2** "The books of the girls" becomes "The girls' books" (more than one owner)

**1** "The boots of the player" becomes "The player's boots" (singular owner)
**but**
**2** "The boots of the players" becomes "The players' boots" (plural owner)

**1** "The leaves of the tree" becomes "The tree's leaves" (singular owner)
**but**
**2** "The leaves of the trees" becomes "The trees' leaves" (plural owner)

If we were to add another **s** in the sentences numbered 2 we would have:
The girls's books The players's boots The trees's leaves

Try and say "girls's", "players's" and "trees's".
It is because these words sound silly that we do not add another **s** when dealing with plural nouns and the apostrophe.

**Exercise 6**

Write out the sentences below, putting in apostrophes where required:

| | | |
|---|---|---|
| 1 | The dogs howls were annoying. | (*one dog*) |
| 2 | The dogs howls were terrifying. | (*seven dogs*) |
| 3 | The triplets clothes are identical. | (*three triplets*) |
| 4 | My sisters boots need mending. | (*two sisters*) |
| 5 | Her friends houses were burgled. | (*one rich friend*) |
| 6 | My teams players are great. | (*only one team*) |
| 7 | The soldiers guns proved useless. | (*many soldiers*) |
| 8 | The armys cause was lost. | (*army is singular*) |
| 9 | The cars tyres were flat. | (*cars is plural*) |
| 10 | My typewriters ribbon has snapped. | (*typewriter is singular*) |

**F** If the plural owners **do not end in** ***s*** we add an apostrophe and **s** to show they possess something.

For example, The men's faces looked weary.
Women's clothes are often expensive.
The children's parents collected them.

**Exercise 7**

Use each of the words below, with an apostrophe, in a sentence:

| | | | | |
|---|---|---|---|---|
| **1** policewoman | **2** chef | **3** dancer | **4** politician | **5** enemy |
| **6** manager | **7** sister | **8** lake | **9** river | **10** general |
| **11** soldier | **12** giraffe | **13** dustman | **14** grocer | **15** buses |
| **16** lorries | **17** cars | **18** trains | **19** runners | **20** nurses |
| **21** nurse | **22** fire | **23** oven | **24** sink | **25** Mrs. Sohal |
| **26** Mr. White | **27** Dr. Samson | **28** people | **29** brother | **30** chief clerk |

**Exercise 8**

Copy out and punctuate this paragraph, putting in apostrophes where they belong.

In his pre match talk Wantgo Uniteds manager warned of the other sides skill. He especially pointed out Browns ability to win tonights game on his own. Our captains opinions were that Citys game could be checked by our defenders hard work. When the referees whistle blew for the start Uniteds defence shattered easily. It was Browns flair which proved to be Citys players main asset. Browns artistic flick to Citys No 11 caused our mens concentration to lapse and we were 1–0 down. Our supporters fears were further justified in the second half by Harris acrobatic goal for City. Uniteds coachs face turned crimson as the whistle blew for the games finish with City beating United 2–0.

# Ferdinand Magellan

Ferdinand Magellan was born at Sabrosa in Portugal in 1480. In his youth he served the Queen and King of Portugal. Portugal at this time was expanding its sea trade to many different parts of the world.

In 1504, Magellan volunteered for a sea voyage to India, where he was wounded in battle. From India he was sent to the East coast of Africa, then back to India, then to Malacca and on to the Spice Islands or Moluccas. These long journeys were made to increase trade and Portuguese influence. Magellan returned to Portugal, only to be sent to Morocco, where he was again wounded in battle. While in Morocco, he was accused of dealing with the enemy and was dismissed by the King.

By now, Magellan was a very experienced soldier and sailor, so he offered his services to the King of Spain. Spain at this time was also trying to build up influence and trade in similar areas to those visited by Portugal.

Magellan wanted to find a route to the Spice Islands by going **west**, instead of east. Columbus had had a similar idea and had discovered the West Indies and the "New World". Magellan wanted to follow the South American coast and find a passage through to the other side. If he could reach the Spice Islands by sailing west he could then return to Spain by sailing right round the world.

Magellan left Spain in 1519 with five ships. He sailed to the Canary Islands and then on to the coast of South America, where he stayed for the winter. He then went south until he found a 580 km passage or strait that led to the great south sea. He named the passage after himself, the Straits of Magellan. The south sea he named the Pacific, because it was so calm and peaceful when he first saw it.

For ninety-eight days, he and his crew sailed across the Pacific Ocean. They ran short of food and water and suffered from the disease scurvy. Even the ships' rats were caught and eaten. At last in 1521, they reached the island of Guam. After resting there they sailed on to the Philippines. Here Magellan tried to help a local ruler and was killed in a fight against some islanders. One of the three sea-worthy ships left was burned, while the other two went on to reach the Spice Islands. These islands were already known from earlier journeys east.

After more difficulties, one of the ships reached Spain. It had sailed round (or circumnavigated) the world – the first ship to achieve this.

Magellan never completed the whole voyage, but he did already know the route from Spain to the Spice Islands going east. He had completed the unknown part of the route round the world – an historic voyage.

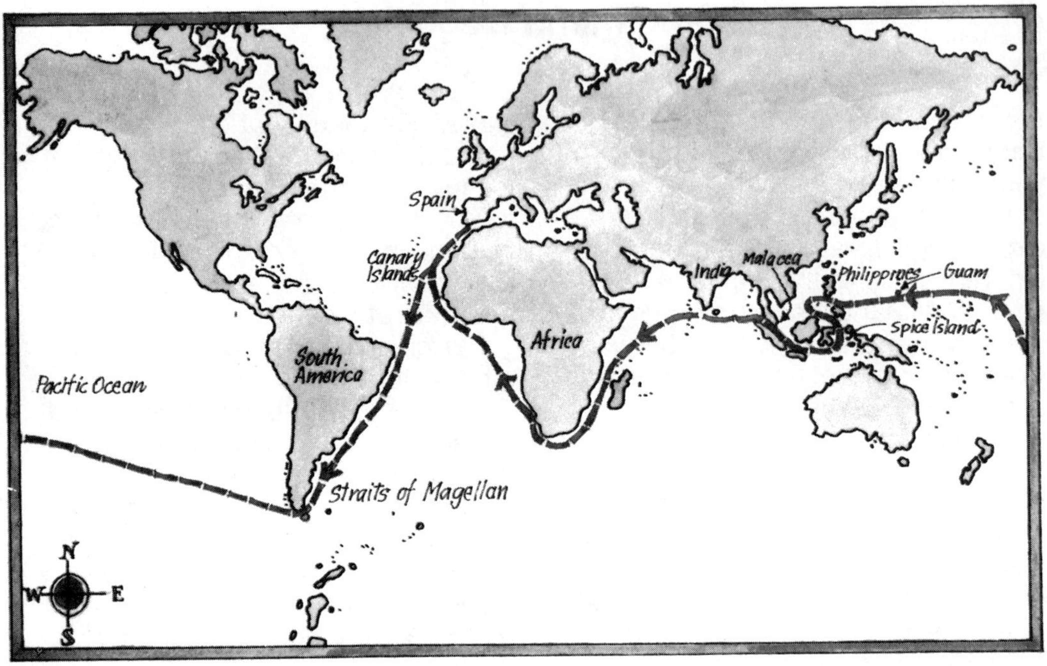


Below you will see a collection of sentences about Magellan. They are not punctuated and they are out of order.

Pick out the sentences, punctuate them and copy them out in the correct order.

Magellan was killed in a fight he reached the great south sea which he named the Pacific he sailed first to the Canary Islands Ferdinand Magellan was born in Portugal in 1480 the men did not have enough food or water one of the ships at last reached Spain he discovered the Straits of Magellan when he was serving the King of Portugal he sailed to India, Malacca and the Spice Islands he wanted to reach the Spice Islands by sailing west he sailed on to the Philippines they suffered from the disease scurvy he left Spain in 1519 they had sailed right round the world at last he arrived at the island of Guam where they rested two of the ships reached the Spice Islands then he reached the coast of South America.

**Dictionary Exercise**
Use each of the following words in a sentence so that its meaning is clear:

| | | | | |
|---|---|---|---|---|
| **1** portable | **2** impressed | **3** separate | **4** conversation | **5** bellow |
| **6** design | **7** solid | **8** liquid | **9** vulnerable | **10** billion |

# Pie Charts

Below you can see five Pie charts. They represent the possible average day of the following people:

an employed adult
a retired senior citizen
a housewife
a pupil
an unemployed adult

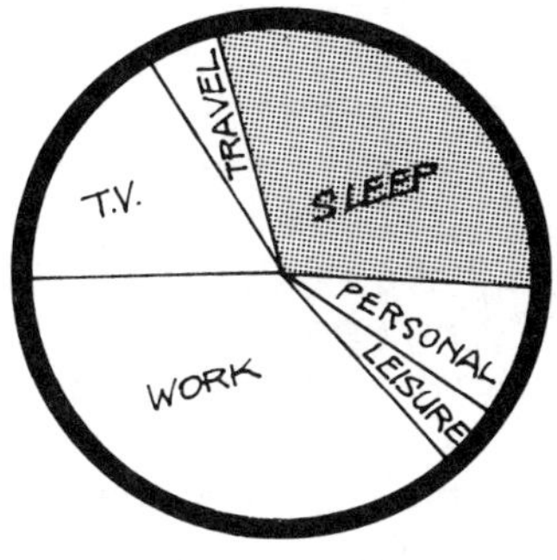


**1 an employed adult**

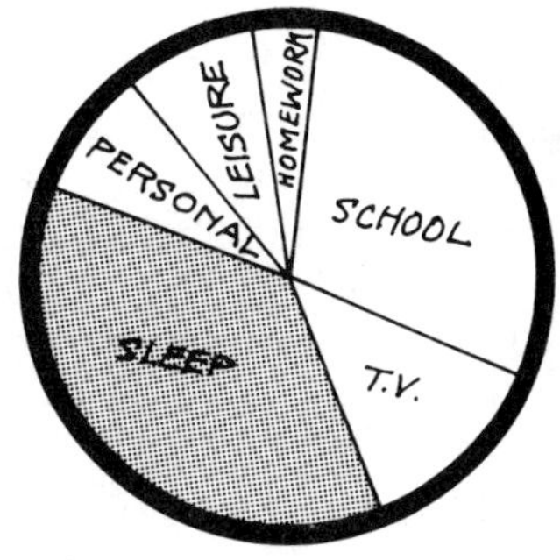


**2 _ _ _ _ _?**

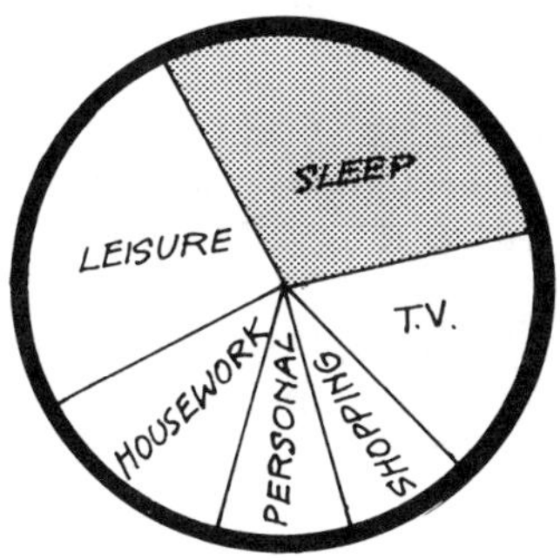


**3 a retired senior citizen**

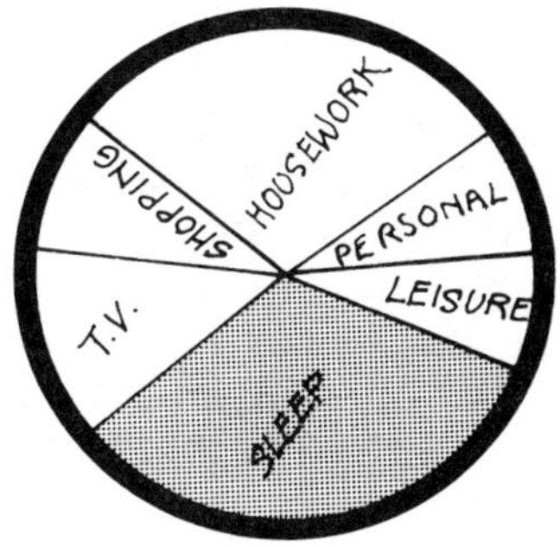


**4 _ _ _ _ _?**

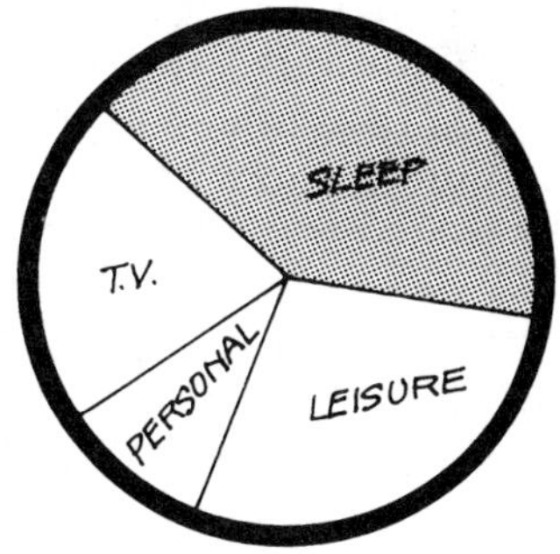


**5 _ _ _ _ _?**

**Exercise 1**

Read this paragraph describing pie chart 1:

The average employed adult sleeps for about seven hours a day. He/she works for nine hours, including breaks, and also takes one hour getting to and from work. Watching television takes up another four hours. That leaves about one hour for other leisure activities and two hours for personal care and eating.

Work out which person each pie chart refers to and write a similar paragraph to the one above for each one.

**Exercise 2**

Make up a questionnaire of your own to check how accurate these charts are. Ask your family and friends how they spend an average weekday.

# Recipe

## Biriani

Well, if you want to make a biriani you'll need about 450 g or 1 lb of cooked lamb. First you have to chop this up and put it in a bowl. Then you add a carton of yoghurt, natural yoghurt, and a couple of teaspoons each of ginger and garlic salt. You mix all this up and leave if for roughly half an hour. Oh, I forgot, you also need 4 or 5 green chillis chopped up. If you can't get them fresh a teaspoon of chilli powder will do. As I said, you leave all this for about 30 minutes.

Next you get the rice ready. You need about 150 g, I think that's about 6 oz, anyway you wash it and then soak it in water for about a quarter of an hour.

After that, you slice up 4 onions thinly and fry them in a little oil. Take half of them out and put them to one side somewhere. Now you tip all that meat mixture into a frying pan, add 2 cups of water and cook it until almost all the water has gone.

Back to the rice now, drain it and put it in a saucepan with 2 cups of water, a bit of salt and a teaspoon each of some spices called cardamom and cinnamon. Boil all this for about 7 minutes and then drain it off.

You're nearly ready now because the rest is easy. You just spread half the rice over the bottom of an oven-proof dish. Then spread the meat mixture over that, then the rest of the rice. You should get 3 layers. On the top put the rest of the onions and a bit of chopped mint.

To finish you've got one last thing to do. Mix half a teaspoon of saffron with hot milk to make a thin paste. Pour this over the lot and put the lid on. Put the dish in a Gas Mark 4 oven, I think that's about 350°F, for 20 minutes. With luck, you should have a delicious hot biriani.

**1** Make a list of the ingredients, mentioned in the recipe above.
For example, 450 g or 1 lb cooked lamb
1 carton natural yoghurt

**2** Make a numbered list of instructions in the right order.
For example, 1 Chop up meat and put it in a bowl
2 Add . . .

# Direct Speech and Speech Marks

Look at this excerpt from the evidence given to Littletown Magistrates Court by P.C. Humphrey:

I was patrolling Saint Street on the evening of 14th May 1983, when I was approached by Sid Grass – the accused. He was acting in a drunken manner, reeling across the pavement and singing. On questioning the accused I discovered that he was, in fact, drunk. I suggested that he go home but he told me, "Leave me alone and get lost, copper!" I told Mr. Grass that his family would be worried about his whereabouts, whereupon he jumped on my back and screamed, "You make me feel as sick as a parrot, go away!" After further heated discussion I was forced to arrest the accused on a charge of drunk and disorderly conduct. When asked if he wished to make a statement the accused said, "Just leave me alone will you?" I warned him that anything he said would be taken down and used in evidence against him. His exact words of reply were, "O.K. It's a fair cop, guvnor. I'm sorry I got so drunk."

**A** There are times when we need to know the **exact words** someone has spoken. In court trials the exact words spoken by a defendent often make the difference between guilty or not guilty judgements. On television and in the newspapers, we are often told exactly what was said by the Prime Minister after an international meeting, by a footballer after winning a medal, by a pop star after holding a successful concert or by a film star who is being sued for divorce. In our own conversations we will repeat what other people say. How often do your friends say "and then I said . . .", "so I said . . ." or "I told her. . . ."?

**Exercise 1**
Write down the four sentences spoken by Sid Grass in the passage above and repeated exactly by P.C. Humphrey.

**B** In magazines and comics writers can show us the exact words spoken by using the form of a cartoon with speech bubbles.

We cannot draw cartoons in our letters, diaries, stories and essays. It would use up far too much space. It looks silly too. Imagine P.C. Humphrey drawing a cartoon each time he had to repeat what Sid Grass had said:

I suggested that he go home but he told me

I told Mr. Grass that his family would be worried about his whereabouts, whereupon he jumped on my back and screamed,

When asked if he wished to make a statement the accused said,

I warned him that anything he said would be taken down and used in evidence against him. His exact words were

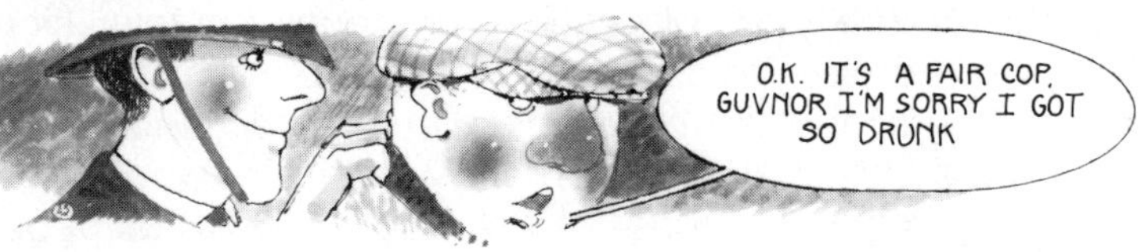


**C** Instead of drawing pictures and speech bubbles in our writing we use speech marks – " ". Speech marks are put around the words that were spoken, and **only** the words that were spoken.

**Exercise 2**
Copy out the words spoken by Sid Grass in the previous passage and place speech marks around them. Put " at the beginning of each sentence he spoke and put " at the end of each of his statements. There are four statements.

Some examples to help you:

| Right | Wrong |
|---|---|
| "What's the time?" he asked. | "What's the time? he asked." |
| "Help!" cried the girl. | "Help! cried the girl." |
| "Hullo," they said. | "Hullo they said." |
| I said "Who are you?" | "I said" Who are you? |

**Exercise 3**
Put speech marks around the words that were spoken by the people in these sentences, copying out each sentence:

**1** You are late again said the teacher.
**2** Where are my shoes? mum asked.
**3** It wasn't my fault cried Eleni.
**4** Isn't it cold? Barry asked.
**5** Come here immediately the teacher roared.
**6** He asked me for some money.
**7** The postman said Good morning, Fiaz.
**8** Jane asked Paul if he had any money.
**9** I told the conductor I've lost my money.
**10** It's a goal he yelled.

**Exercise 4**
Write one sentence for what you would say in each of the following situations. Remember to use speech marks.

For example, to a bus conductor when you had forgotten your fare.
"I've left my money at home," I told the conductor.

**1** to your favourite singer
**2** to a policewoman at midnight
**3** to a tramp asking for money
**4** to your mum when she got your school report
**5** to an injured cyclist
**6** to a teacher asking for your homework
**7** to your dad when you got home late
**8** to a burglar in your flat
**9** to a five-year-old with a new chemistry set
**10** to a friend who has scratched your favourite record.

**D** There are three ways of writing down speech.

**The first way**

"Be quiet or else you'll stay in!" the teacher shouted

the actual words spoken | who spoke | how spoken

In this case the spoken words come first and are followed by the words that tell us who spoke and how the words were spoken.

"I've lost my bus fare," the little boy cried

the actual words spoken | who spoke | how spoken

"Where are my keys?" Dad asked

the actual words spoken | who spoke | how spoken

**Exercise 5**

Put the speech marks in the correct place in these sentences, copying out each sentence:

**1** I think I'll call this place America said Columbus.
**2** Why's that? asked a passing Indian.
**3** Can you think of another name? Columbus quietly asked.
**4** That's an awful name, sneered the Indian.
**5** Look, I've come a long way and had a lousy trip Columbus shouted.
**6** There's no need to get angry with me, the Indian answered.
**7** I'm sorry, apologised Columbus.
**8** That's all right. I guess it's been a long day, agreed the Indian.
**9** Yes! America will be the name of this new land, smiled Columbus.
**10** What do you mean by that nonsense? We've been living here for centuries, called the Indian as he walked away.

**The second way**
The second method of writing down speech is to have the actual words spoken last in the sentence:

Sunil shouted, "Watch out, Jim!"

who spoke and how → the actual words spoken

The angry girl screamed at Tom, "Leave me alone!"

who spoke → how spoken → the actual words spoken

The carpenter asked, "Who's got my hammer?"

who spoke → how spoken → the actual words spoken

**Exercise 6**
Put the speechmarks in the correct place in these sentences, copying out each one:

1 Caveman Ugh said to Yuk, Light the fire.
2 Yuk, looked up and asked, Where are the matches?
3 Ugh got angry and shouted, We haven't invented matches yet.
4 Yuk demanded, Why not?
5 Ugh was getting more annoyed and shouted, You're a fool.
6 Yuk was fed up too and he moaned, How can I light a fire, then?
7 Feeling sorry for Yuk, Ugh said Go down to the shop and buy a lighter.
8 Yuk grumbled, It's too cold and the shop is miles away.
9 Ugh suggested, Get a bus, then.
10 Yuk replied, They haven't been invented yet.

**The third way**

"No matter how hard I try," the girl mumbled, "I can't do it."

the actual words spoken — who spoke and how — the actual words spoken

In this method of presenting speech the words spoken are interrupted by the words telling us who spoke and how the words were spoken. These words are followed by more speech from the same person.

"If you could help," he whispered, "I'll try once more."

the actual words spoken — who spoke and how — the actual words spoken

"Put your hands up," the thief shouted, "or I'll shoot!"

the actual words spoken — who spoke and how — the actual words spoken

**Exercise 7**

It is said that Sir Francis Drake continued his game of bowls when the Spanish Armada of 130 ships attacked England.

Put the speech marks in the correct place in this imaginary conversation between Drake and his friend, copying out each sentence:

1. Captain, the sailor said, what's that noise?
2. No idea, Drake replied, but it may be the Armada.
3. What's the score now?, the sailor asked. Am I winning?
4. I'll never lose to you! Drake roared, The Armada can wait!
5. Liz will be angry, the sailor smirked, she doesn't like the Armada.
6. I've got a pound on this game, said Drake, and I intend to win it.
7. Those noises, the sailor stuttered, they sound like guns.
8. Who cares? snapped Captain Drake. It's only the Spanish.
9. We must fight, quipped the sailor, it's not our day off.
10. Oh, sighed Drake, in that case we'll call this game a draw.

# Answers

Page 3 **Ex. 1** English, French, Geography, Mathematics, Science

**Ex. 2** Bach, Bartok, Beethoven, Bellini, Berlioz, Brahms, Britten

**Ex. 3** Norfolk, Northamptonshire, Northumberland, Nottinghamshire, Somerset, Suffolk, Surrey, Sussex

**Ex. 4** Salisbury, Southend, Southport, Southwold, Stafford, Stirling, Stockport, Stoke, Stranraer, Sunderland, Swansea

**Ex. 5** **For example:** pearl, postman, Peru, polo, Portsmouth, pike, parrot, pig, pea, pansy, pink, pear, pine, Paula, Perry

Page 5 **Ex. 1** **1.** study **2.** flows **3.** falls **4.** flows **5.** is mined **6.** load, unload **7.** is **8.** is **9.** separates **10.** consists

**Ex. 2** apply, beat, catch, draw, eat, fall, go, hold, ignore, jump, kill, love, moan, need, open, play, queue, rise, sit, tear, undo, view, walk, x-ray, yell, zoom

Page 6 **Ex. 4** **1.** desert **2.** wide **3.** hide **4.** amaze **5.** impolite **6.** sprint **7.** unoccupied **8.** ape **9.** said **10.** roared

Page 7 **Ex. 1** **1.** the **2.** London, of **3.** The, in **4.** is, from **5.** of, has, than **6.** are, in **7.** e.g. are, reared, in **8.** from, to, and **9.** used, coal **10.** e.g. and, are, in, parts

Page 8 **Ex. 2**

**2.** There are many small islands off the Scottish coast.
**3.** The north of Scotland has many mountains.
**4.** Ben Nevis is the highest mountain.
**5.** Most people live in the lowland area.
**6.** Coal is mined near Glasgow.
**7.** The capital city of Scotland is Edinburgh.
**8.** Fishing is important in the east of Scotland.
**9.** Lakes in Scotland are known as lochs.
**10.** The River Spey is the longest Scottish river.

**Ex. 3**

You will need 4 oz minced beef, onion, salt, pepper.
Melt the butter in a pan.
Fry the onion in the pan.
Mix the onion with the mince.
Mix in the salt and pepper.
Pat the mixture into a round shape.
Fry the mixture until it is cooked.
Toast a roll or bun.
Place the hamburger inside the roll.

Page 9 **Ex. 5**

**1.** The founder of the Moslem religion was Mohammed. He was born some time between the years 570 and 580 A.D. in Mecca.
**2.** Mohammed was brought up by his grandfather and uncle. He emerged as a prophet when he was forty.
**3.** He stated the existence of one god. The name of this god was Allah. The religious leaders of Mecca did not accept Mohammed's message.
**4.** He fled 200 miles to Medina. Here he became a religious, political and military leader. In 630 his army conquered Mecca.
**5.** He rebuilt the sacred temple. He established Medina as the capital of the new Moslem state. The Arabian chiefs vowed allegiance.
**6.** The bible of Islam is the Koran. It consists of the things Allah was said to have spoken to Mohammed. It was not written down until after his death. The Koran consists of 200,000 words. It is divided into fourteen chapters.
**7.** Allah is also called the Hearer and the Guide. He is complete master of the Universe. Allah created the earth and heaven in six days. He will judge each person on the Day of Judgement.
**8.** Jesus Christ appears in the Koran as a prophet. He was a messenger of Allah. The Koran insists Allah had no son. Jesus is just a man.
**9.** Prayer is an essential part of the Moslem religion. It takes place five times a day. A Moslem faces Mecca when praying.
**10.** Fasting takes place during Ramadan. This is the ninth lunar month of the year. A Moslem should visit Mecca at least once in his life.

Page 10 **Ex. 6** When I was very young my parents left me for dead in a strange place. There was hardly a sign of life in me. Then a kind stranger found me. She protected me, clothed and fed me as if I was one of her own children. She cared for me until I grew up. When I was fully grown I left. She lost her own sons and daughters because she helped me.

The bird is a cuckoo.

Page 12 **Ex. 1** **1.** Regent's Park **2.** Marble Arch

Page 13 **Ex. 2** **For example:**

**1.** When did the Romans first come to Britain?
**2.** Who led them?
**3.** To what point in the north did the Romans rule Britain?
**4.** What was Hadrian's Wall?
**5.** Who opposed the Romans?
**6.** Why was the Romans' hold on Britain weakened?
**7.** When did the Romans abandon Britain?
**8.** What positive features did the Romans leave in Britain?
**9.** How can you recognise Roman towns?
**10.** Where is there a Roman bath and theatre?

Page 14 **Ex. 3** **1.** 7 **2.** 5 **3.** Physical Education and Religious Education **4.** 23 hours 20 minutes **5.** Art **6.** It is a practical subject with lots of preparation and clearing up **7.** Physical Education **8.** 65 minutes **9.** Wednesday **10.** Tuesday

Page 15 **Ex. 6**

| **strings** | **brass** | **percussion** | **wind** | **keyboards** |
|---|---|---|---|---|
| viola | trombone | drums | oboe | piano |
| violin | saxaphone | cymbals | bassoon | organ |
| cello | trumpet | triangle | clarinet | harpsichord |
| double bass | french horn | tympani | flute | |
| guitar | cornet | tambourine | | |

Page 16 **Ex. 1** Help

**Ex. 2** When you see or hear a message how do you know when a letter or word ends and the next letter or word begins?

**Ex. 4** **1.** Telegram **2.** Too much

Page 18 **Ex. 4** William I, also known as William the Conqueror, was King of England, 1066 to 1087. He was the son of Robert, Duke of Normandy. William emerged from a long struggle with the King of France with control of Normandy and other territories. He had been promised the English throne by his cousin Edward the Confessor and by Harold who had been shipwrecked in France. When Harold was proclaimed King of England William invaded England. At the Battle of Hastings in October 1066 Harold was killed and the Normans were victorious. The story of the Norman Conquest is told, from the Norman point of view, in the Bayeux Tapestry. On Christmas Day William was crowned King of England in Westminster Abbey. England was not totally subdued for another five years until the defeat of Hereward the Wake.

Page 19 **Ex. 1** **1.** horses **2.** cats **3.** dogs **4.** pets **5.** bees **6.** elephants **7.** giraffes **8.** dolphins **9.** lions **10.** tortoises

**Ex. 2** **1.** armies **2.** industries **3.** counties **4.** plays **5.** cities **6.** centuries **7.** countries **8.** days **9.** monkeys **10.** energies

**Ex. 3** **1.** wives **2.** knives **3.** shelves **4.** leaves **5.** halves **6.** loaves **7.** lives **8.** elves **9.** wolves **10.** scarves

Page 20 **Ex. 4** **1.** dishes **2.** switches **3.** kisses **4.** addresses **5.** sixes **6.** classes **7.** watches **8.** buzzes **9.** boxes **10.** ashes

**Ex. 5** **1.** child **2.** tooth **3.** woman **4.** sheep **5.** die **6.** potato **7.** foot **8.** chief **9.** goose **10.** piano

**Ex. 6** ACROSS: **1.** flies **6.** arms **9.** leaves **12.** hoe **14.** ass **15.** vet **16.** men **17.** s **18.** sip
DOWN: **2.** loaves **3.** elms **4.** taxes **5.** eel **7.** reds **8.** shelves **10.** es **11.** alarm **13.** spy **19.** tap

Page 22 **Ex. 2** The past tense of the verbs:
**1.** roared **2.** screamed **3.** annoyed **4.** scratched **5.** enjoyed **6.** detested **7.** collected **8.** started **9.** destroyed **10.** suggested

**Ex. 3** The past tense of the verbs:
**1.** hoped **2.** liked **3.** teased **4.** hired **5.** described **6.** noticed **7.** starved **8.** scared **9.** swerved **10.** accelerated

Page 23 **Ex. 4** The past tense of the verbs:
**1.** blotted **2.** grabbed **3.** hopped **4.** begged **5.** shopped **6.** stopped **7.** knitted **8.** skidded **9.** ripped **10.** capped

**Ex. 5** The past tense of the verbs:
**1.** carried **2.** supplied **3.** spied **4.** applied **5.** replied **6.** denied **7.** studied **8.** worried **9.** copied **10.** satisfied

**Ex. 6**

| | | | |
|---|---|---|---|
| drink | drank | buy | bought |
| sit | sat | bring | brought |
| put | put | catch | caught |
| cut | cut | fight | fought |
| sing | sang | do | did |
| ring | rang | get | got |
| fly | flew | give | gave |
| know | knew | dig | dug |
| grow | grew | see | saw |
| throw | threw | speak | spoke |
| draw | drew | swear | swore |
| win | won | write | wrote |
| read | read | eat | ate |
| run | ran | is | was |
| lose | lost | choose | chose |

Page 24 **Ex. 8** ACROSS: **1.** was **3.** signalled **8.** tie **9.** dropped **11.** walked **14.** sat **16.** nodded **17.** grew **20.** did **21.** stopped **24.** dealt **26.** rained **29.** grow **30.** trap
DOWN: **1.** were **2.** said **4.** note **5.** let **6.** dreamt **7.** sped **10.** designed **11.** went **12.** led **13.** erect **15.** tied **18.** will **19.** ape **21.** sang **22.** dent **23.** fry **25.** tap **27.** er **28.** do

Page 26

Marco Polo was born in Venice around the year 1253. His father was a merchant. His father had been to China. They wanted to return to Cathay to try to open up safe routes and control the trade between Cathay and Europe. Marco's journey began in 1271. He travelled from Venice to Acre by ship, then overland to Hormuz, across Persia into the Gobi Desert and then to Shangtu. The journey took four years. It was a long and dangerous journey. Kublai Khan ruled that part of Asia. Marco studied the language and became a sort of ambassador. He stayed for thirteen years. He returned to Venice in 1295. He had been away for 24 years. At first no-one believed his stories. The people learned about the people, animals and lands of Asia. Marco Polo died in 1324.

Page 29 **Ex. 1** apricot, gooseberry, grape, grapefruit, peach, pear, plum, prune, raisin, raspberry

**Ex. 2** broccoli, cabbage, celery, cucumber, pea, potato, radish, spinach, sprout, swede

**Ex. 3** haddock, hake, halibut, herring, salmon, sardine, scampi, shrimp, skate, sole

**A Ex. 1** C.G. Green, H.S. Green, M.P. Green, P.L. Green, W.B. Green

**Ex. 2** C.A. Carter, C.C. Carter, C.D. Carter, C.H. Carter, C.V. Carter

Page 30 **Ex. 3** B.M. Wind, B.P. Wind, C.D. Wind, L.T. Wine, L.V. Wine, M.M. Wine, M.A. Winter, M.L. Winter, M.V. Winter

**Ex. 4**
**1. a)** 01 . . .5372 **b)** 01 . . .8223 **c)** 01 . . .7121 **d)** 01 . . .3219
**2. a)** 68 Harvey Gdns SE7 **b)** 104 Verdun Rd SW13 **c)** 53 Boileau Rd W5 **d)** 22 Chelwood, Oakleigh Rd Nth N20
**3. a)** 01 . . .3851 **b)** 01 . . .0575 **c)** 01 . . .7395
**4.** They are in the London area.
**5.** Snowdon Snowden or Soan Soane.

**B**
**7.** Avenue, Street, Gardens, Square, House, Close, Crescent, Lane, Grove, Park, Court
**8. a)** Newsagent **b)** Furniture manufacturer

Page 32 **Ex. 1** **1.** I am **2.** he is **3.** could not **4.** should not **5.** do not **6.** she is **7.** did not **8.** is not **9.** was not **10.** must not

**Ex. 2** **1.** what's **2.** there's **3.** who's **4.** where's **5.** here's **6.** aren't **7.** weren't **8.** hasn't **9.** they're **10.** we're

**A Ex. 3** **1.** I will **2.** you will **3.** he will **4.** she will **5.** they will **6.** we will **7.** cannot **8.** could have **9.** I have **10.** you have

**Ex. 4** **1.** it'll **2.** they've **3.** would've **4.** should've **5.** we've **6.** you've **7.** she'll **8.** I'll **9.** could've **10.** might've

Page 35

**1.** Where was Christopher Columbus born?
**2.** What did he want to find?
**3.** To whom did he present his idea?
**4.** How long did it take him to persuade people to support him?
**5.** When did he set sail?
**6.** What were the three ships called?
**7.** Which islands did he reach first?
**8.** When did they sight land?
**9.** What was the land called?
**10.** Who had reached America earlier?
**11.** When did he arrive back in Spain?
**12.** What happened to him when he returned to Spain?
**13.** Did he ever return to America? *or* How many times did he go back to the "New World"?
**14.** When and where did he die?

Page 39 **Ex. 1** **1.** hot cold **2.** north south **3.** cool warm **4.** dawn dusk **5.** east west **6.** left right **7.** barren fertile **8.** sunrise sunset **9.** shallow deep **10.** smooth rough

**Ex. 2** **1.** finish **2.** whisper **3.** succeed **4.** fall **5.** come **6.** remember **7.** lose **8.** depart **9.** cool **10.** drop

**Ex. 3** **1.** happy **2.** clean **3.** black **4.** incorrect **5.** short **6.** thin **7.** tiny **8.** noisy **9.** young **10.** new

**Ex. 4** **1.** happiness **2.** child **3.** freedom **4.** night, nightime **5.** morning **6.** hate **7.** back **8.** beginning **9.** good **10.** foreground

**A Ex. 5** **1.** untied **2.** unkind **3.** unlucky **4.** imperfect **5.** unclear **6.** regular **7.** competent **8.** possible **9.** likely **10.** soluble

Page 40 **Ex. 1**

Most people in India are Hindus. Over 300 million people practise the Hindu religion. The Hindus worship many gods and have many images of them. These gods are different ways of speaking about one god. This spirit is called Brahman. Prayer is performed alone. There are few great festivals where people worship together. There are many holy books. The three most important ones are the Vedas, Upanishads and Gita.

**Ex. 2**

A mammal is a vertebrate animal, meaning it has a backbone. A mammal is usually covered with hair, wool or fur. It is warm-blooded. A mammal does not lay eggs, it gives birth to live young. It feeds its young with milk. A mammal that eats meat is called a carnivore. A mammal that eats plants is called a herbivore. A mammal that eats plants and meat is called an omnivore.

Mammals are vertebrate animals, meaning they have a backbone. Mammals are usually covered with hair, wool or fur. They are warm-blooded. Mammals do not lay eggs, they give birth to live young. They feed their young with milk. Mammals that eat meat are called carnivores. Mammals that eat plants are called herbivores. Mammals that eat plants and meat are called omnivores.

**Ex. 3** accept–refuse increase–decrease lengthen–shorten pleasure–pain honest–dishonest deep–shallow west–east enemy–ally victory–defeat sadness–happiness defend–attack yes–no purchase–sell hinder–help honesty–dishonesty contract–expand infertile–fertile freeze–thaw impossible–possible cool–warm

Page 41

In 1910 Captain R. Scott left England in the ship Terra Nova. He sailed to Antarctica to investigate the Ross Sea area and to try to reach the South Pole. Scott's Party set up a base on the west of Ross Island. Scott set out with motor sledges, ponies and dogs. Scott's motor-sledges soon broke down, the ponies were shot and later even the dog teams were sent back. Exhausted and pulling the sledges themselves, Scott's team reached the South Pole on January 17th 1912. Blizzards, exhaustion and a shortage of fuel finally beat Scott and his men. They died still a long way from their base. Their bodies were found on November 12th 1912.

In 1910 Roald Amundsen sailed from Norway to Antarctica in the ship Fram. He had intended to go to the North Pole but someone else had got there first, so he decided to try for the South Pole. Amundsen's party set up a base in the Bay of Whales on the Ross Ice Shelf. Amundsen set out with four companions on October 20th 1911. Amundsen took sledges and fifty-two dogs. He reached the South Pole on December 14th. Amundsen and his men returned safely in thirty-eight days and had twelve dogs left.

Page 42

Paragraph 1 his=Richard's; He=John; He=John; they=his barons; he=John; he=John; any=any of his barons; their=the barons'

Paragraph 2 him=John; them=the barons; he=John; this=the Great Charter

Paragraph 3 him=John

Paragraph 4 their=John's and the barons'; them=the barons; him=John

Page 43

There are over six million Sikhs in the world mostly living in the Punjab region of India where the Sikh religion began. Sikh men are easily distinguished as they always have beards and wear turbans.

The sacred book of the Sikh religion is the Granth. It is a collection of the teachings of a number of people. The various teachings were brought together by Arjun. He lived from 1563 until 1606. The Granth is written in Punjabi. The Granth is composed of hymns. These are set to music and chanted each day in the Sikh temples.

The Granth includes hymns by many Indian teachers. Most are Sikhs but there are also verses by Hindu and Moslem holy men. There were ten great teachers of the Sikhs. These masters are known as gurus. After the tenth teacher died the Granth became the Sikh guru. Now it would guide them.

Page 44 **Ex. 4** triangular – triangle; circular – circle; semi-circular – semi-circle; spherical – sphere; rectangular – rectangle; oval – oval; hexagonal – hexagon; conical – cone; pentagonal – pentagon; square – square; septagonal – septagon; cylindrical – cylinder; octagonal – octagon

Page 45 **Ex. 1** **2.** mother, Deborah **3.** cat, Margaret **4.** core, apple **5.** bicycle, father **6.** dog, Susan **7.** shop, Mrs. Jones **8.** house, Satnam **9.** dictionary, Eleni **10.** leaves, tree

Page 46 **Ex. 2** **1.** Jim's **2.** Jane's **3.** Kuldip's **4.** Manjit's **5.** Clive's **6.** Laurel's **7.** Eleni's **8.** Lena's **9.** Harjeet's **10.** Mandeep's

**Ex. 3** **1.** The dog's owner **2.** oven's temperature **3.** fisherman's nets **4.** sun's rays **5.** girl's party **6.** policeman's job **7.** Mr. Singh's son **8.** tiger's claws **9.** pilot's face **10.** boxer's gloves

Page 48 **Ex. 4** Marlene's **1.** hair **2.** throat, neck **3.** tennis racket **4.** watch **5.** book **6.** eye **7.** back, blouse **8.** thigh, skirt **9.** foot, shoe **10.** ankle, sock

The horse's **1.** forehead **2.** eye **3.** mouth **4.** hoof **5.** belly **6.** leg **7.** tail **8.** back **9.** saddle **10.** neck

Page 49 **Ex. 5** **1.** Lloyd's **2.** Car's **3.** horse's **4.** dog's **5.** — **6.** tiger's **7.** mother's **9.** teacher's **9.** book's **10.** John's

Page 50 **Ex. 6** **1.** dog's **2.** dogs' **3.** triplets' **4.** sisters' **5.** friend's **6.** team's **7.** soldiers' **8.** army's **9.** cars' **10.** typewriter's

**Ex. 8** In his pre-match talk Wantgo United's manager warned of the other side's skill. He especially pointed out Brown's ability to win tonight's game on his own. Our captain's opinions were that City's game could be checked by our defenders' hard work. When the referee's whistle blew for the start, United's defence shattered easily. It was Brown's flair which proved to be City's players' main asset. Brown's artistic flick to City's No 11 caused our men's concentration to lapse and we were 1–0 down. Our supporters' fears were further justified in the second half by Harris's acrobatic goal for City. United's coach's face turned crimson as the whistle blew for the game's finish with City beating United 2–0.

Page 52

Ferdinand Magellan was born in Portugal in 1480. When he was serving the King of Portugal he sailed to India, Malacca and the Spice Islands.

He wanted to reach the Spice Islands by sailing west. He left Spain in 1519. He sailed first to the Canary Islands. Then he reached the coast of South America. He discovered the Straits of Magellan. He reached the great south sea which he named the Pacific. The men did not have enough food or water. They suffered from the disease scurvy. At last he arrived at the island of Guam where they rested. He sailed on to the Philippines. Magellan was killed in a fight. Two of the ships reached the Spice Islands. One of the ships at last reached Spain. They had sailed right round the world.

Page 53 **Ex. 1** **2.** Pupil **4.** Housewife **5.** Unemployed adult